Colours of Loneliness
and Other Stories

Colours of Loneliness
and Other Stories

PARAMITA SATPATHY

Translated from Odia by
SNEHAPRAVA DAS

Edited by
MINI KRISHNAN

OXFORD
UNIVERSITY PRESS

OXFORD
UNIVERSITY PRESS

Oxford University Press is a department of the University of Oxford.
It furthers the University's objective of excellence in research, scholarship,
and education by publishing worldwide. Oxford is a registered trademark of
Oxford University Press in the UK and in certain other countries.

Published in India by
Oxford University Press
2/11 Ground Floor, Ansari Road, Daryaganj, New Delhi 110 002, India

© Oxford University Press 2019

The moral rights of the authors have been asserted.

First Edition published in 2019

ISBN-13 (print edition): 978-0-19-949456-9
ISBN-10 (print edition): 0-19-949456-8

ISBN-13 (eBook): 978-0-19-909756-2
ISBN-10 (eBook): 0-19-909756-9

Typeset in Trump Mediaeval LT Std 10/16
by Tranistics Data Technologies, New Delhi 110 044
Printed in India by Rakmo Press, New Delhi 110 020

Contents

Author's Note

I live two lives, one visible to others, for others, and the other only for me. I collect ingredients from the life that is for others and offer those to the life that is mine. I often endure the pangs and ecstasies of duality. I have come to terms with the realization that I am abnormal. I am abnormal because the general facts and figures of life tempt me to transform them to something which I feel they ought to be.

Since time immemorial, I have been enchanted with short stories. They pose irresistible pouches of mystery before me—dark, deep, intense, crisp, and succulent. I do not exactly remember when this line of charm got blurred and I entered the arena. Like a sudden lightening in the sky, a gush of shower on a hot summer day, like a finger bleeding from an unintended cut—a splotch-like something enters me. It stays in me for some time, swells in me. Then comes out a convoy of words, leaving me spellbound. At that moment, I come face to face with aloneness—shuddering and shivering on its impact. Strange that this experience comes back to me again and again....

In my stories, I try to paint the spectrum of life in its strange hues—such bewildering revelations that unsettle me. From the raging swirl of my experiences, I try to stretch the thread that connects to an ever-elusive vision we keep chasing ceaselessly but have never been able to strike a chord with. Critics often hold that my stories are a crusade against patriarchy. May be because most of the protagonists of my stories are women who are in search of space for themselves. I cannot help being bitten by the quest of these women either.

They say that short stories are dominating today's literary scene because they are short, take a small slice of time of the readers, letting them disengage quickly. I do not subscribe to this. I guess short stories are adored because they ignite immediate passion in the reader and leave the reader still wanting more, although the stories have stopped telling themselves long since. Short stories have an amazing ability to disintegrate a rather complex perception to a simple happening.

I am privileged to read some of the finest stories written in Indian languages and am proud to state that they are no less powerful than those of any other language of the world. In my language, too, great stories have been crafted. I often feel that there is probably nothing new I can create. What I wish to say might have already been told or is being written in some corner of the world at the moment. I have reconciled that my job is to narrate it my way.

I am aware that transforming the stories to this language of the world while keeping the form of expression intact is not at all an easy job. The relentless endeavour of Snehaprava towards rendering the stories in English has left me awestruck. The role of Mini Krishnan in waving her magic wand of editing and making this metamorphosis happen goes beyond mundane appreciation. I can never be adequately indebted to both.

I shall always remember the efforts of Bikram Das in the correction of the draft and for writing the introduction to the book. I thank Jatin Nayak and Himanshu Mohapatra for their valuable inputs in the making of the book. I take this occasion to thank Oxford University Press for publishing this collection; for the perseverance of the team for being with the script day in and day out and for making this happen. I also thank the readers of the stories whose response encouraged me to create yet another.

Paramita Satpathy

Translator's Note

A translation from a regional language like Odia into an international language like English becomes a product of the reception of the influence of the original on the translator. It is even more so in the case of Paramita Satpathy's stories, which have a rootedness in the soil of Odisha. It is a challenging task to recreate the changing graphics of her language pattern that keeps switching from colloquial to sophisticated, from slangy to suave. She handles the jargon and maxims with quite an expertise, satisfying the need of her themes. Her style, depending upon the demands of the mood in her stories, could be racy or reserved, flowing or laconic, narrative or symbolic. While weaving the language into the fabric of her style, she maintains a logical balance to form a regular pattern.

The translator, an individual creative writer herself, is compelled by her creative instincts not to let her own voice get smothered all the time under the pressing demand of preserving fidelity to the original writing. The element of transparency, therefore, at certain stages, is influenced by the needs of the language she uses. Since a translator's strategy is often conditioned by the nature of the text to be translated, while at the task of translating the stories of Paramita into

English, this translator was forced to take a little liberty here and there to reproduce the effect that the original text intends to make on the reader. There is always the risk of rendering recreated text dull and flat if the translator limits their efforts to just inventing a corresponding mode of expression or grafting the ethnicity of Odia culture into the language structure of English.

The stories chosen for translation cover a broad range of subjects and address some of the typical issues relating to human values as well as social customs. 'Children's Day' is a moving tale of a slum boy working in a sweetmeat shop who falls victim to the perverted and brutal passion of his employer. Utterly helpless and driven by a desperate desire to escape the consuming agony perpetrated on him, he, in the end, is compelled to kill his abuser. Paramita Satpathy's stories hold out a cross-section of the typical Indian middle-class sociocultural ethos, where the protagonists struggle desperately to survive the challenges of an oppressive system.

A different story, 'The N-Club', exposes the bitter emptiness at the bottom of the ostentatious aristocracy we love to flaunt. 'A Fable for the Times' and 'The Elixir of Love' are tales where the author, like an experienced mind-reader, delves deep into the human subconscious by creating a dream-like atmosphere that seems to have a Gothic eeriness about it. In 'Wild Jasmine', she ventures out to expose the shocking reality of the plans undertaken by the government to benefit the poor and the downtrodden, and the humiliation and atrocity inflicted upon defenceless humanity, while 'The Nowhere Nest' delineates a woman's futile quest for identity in a world ruled by male supremacist ideology that denies her a sense of belonging. 'A Real Diamond!' recounts the silent, secret longing of a woman for the bliss of love. 'Her Best Friend Jaya' is still another shocker that reveals an altogether different facet of the woman and portrays her as a seductress who compromises with her feminine dignity to achieve her end.

Paramita's stories have an appeal that sinks straight into the senses and evokes a response so pure and genuine that readers are compelled to accept the experience of the characters as their own, completely ignoring any element of alienation that might have been there to keep them out of the orbit. Just think of the dream world the reader is transported to on the wings of the author's fancy in 'The Girl from a Foreign Land' and have the feel of that tender sensuousness! It is all about the angst, the hopeless craving of bridled passion buried under the unfathomed depth of the heart, to be set free. A class apart is 'Jungle Lore', that uses the jungle scene as a perfect ambience for the surfacing of the crude animalism concealed carefully under the veneer of sophistication. At the same time, it is a bold rejection of male dominancy that takes the submissive role of a woman for granted.

An obsession with guilt, penitence, revenge, and rebellion seems to be systemic to Paramita's thematic and stylistic experimentation. In 'A Shadow in the Mirror', the author has woven an intricate web by superimposing the past over the present through flashback, introspection, a secret self-condemnation, and simple straightforward third-person narration. The protagonist is haunted by the memory of the terrible guilt of pulling an innocent prank that made him lose his elder brother. Oft and on, the sense of guilt keeps returning to him, every time with multiplied intensity to invade the world of complacence he desperately needs to protect through his conscious efforts. 'The Unborn Daughter's Story' is a lone woman's crusade against the cold and ruthless patriarchal values that feminine sentiments are always crushed under. By killing her unborn daughter, she challenges the very act of the creation of a life.

The reader's attention is instantly drawn to the dichotomy of longing and belonging, of desire and disillusionment, in 'Colours of Loneliness', a poignant story of two close friends, who journeyed along the two different paths destiny had chartered for them—and 'that has made all the difference', if we are to recall Frost[1]—reaching a point where 'living' proves to be an exercise in futility. The hope and despair juxtaposed with fine, artistic décor, and the subtle melancholy and dignity of expression are tempting enough to seek a semblance to the delicate yet sombre Maupassant ambience in the story.

It is the need of the time that voices such as of Paramita Satpathy should reach far. The honest and inhibition-free attitude with which she addresses sociocultural issues and the impartial judgement of human behaviour that lends force and charm to her stories are the marks of a promising writer. While translating Paramita's stories to English, I strived to transfer her thoughts with equal honesty and fairness, always aiming at doing justice to her writing. The pleasure will be all mine if the stories rendered in English can find a space in the reader's heart.

Snehaprava Das

[1] Robert Frost, 'The Road Not Taken', 1916.

Introduction

Paramita Satpathy Tripathy (b. 1965) belongs to the second generation of modern writers of fiction in Odia, following in the wake of masters like Gopinath Mohanty, Kishori Charan Das, and Manoj Das (to name only three). In the duration spanning more than three decades for which she has been writing, Paramita has carved out a niche for herself, with seven collections of short stories and three novels to her credit. Several of her stories have been translated into English, Hindi, and other Indian languages and published in leading periodicals as well as in book form. She has received the prestigious Central Sahitya Akademi award and several other literary honours.

Like many other writers of her generation, Paramita bridges the traditional and the contemporary. Her stories are carefully crafted and satisfy most canons of the classic short story, but they also have the fluidity and freedom of modern fiction.

The Odia short story is said to have originated in Fakir Mohan Senapati's 'Rebati', the tragic saga of a young girl who faces social persecution because of her passion for education. This pioneering work, produced more than 150 years ago, foreshadows several of Paramita's concerns as a writer, which are reflected also in some folk legends prevalent in Odisha that depict the suffering of the girl child. Prominent among them is the *Tapoi* legend, which is connected with an important Odia festival. However, women have not always appeared to the Odia imagination as helpless and subservient creatures. In every Odia home is preserved the myth of the *Lakshmi Purana*, which tells the story of how Lakshmi, the goddess of wealth, crushes the male ego of her lord and master, Jagannath, and his brother Balaram, denying them food until they seek her forgiveness. This is an acknowledgement of the primacy of the female not only in the home but also in the cosmic order. Several of Paramita's stories are a tribute to the inherent resilience and strength of women.

Being a woman herself, intensely aware of the indignities that women suffer in a male-dominated society, Paramita would inevitably have responded strongly to the feminine experience. Yet she does not accept the label 'feminist' that is often thrust on her. 'I do not necessarily represent the woman's point of view,' she mentions, 'but I do have a woman's imagination and see the world as a woman.'[1]

Paramita is committed in equal measure to her art and her ideology. 'It has always been important for me to tell a good story,' she says, 'but I firmly believe that no form of art can exist without a vision. Most of my stories have begun as a feeling that flashes across my mind and grows on me. I try weaving a plot around it. I write about things that I have felt intensely about and attempt to express that part of women's lives which is often buried and endured in silence. It doesn't matter to me whether a clear message, political, social or moral, comes out of it or not.'[2]

[1] Personal conversation with Paramita Satpathy.
[2] Personal conversation with Paramita Satpathy.

Paramita's fiction is rooted in social reality: most of her characters, particularly her women, are people that we meet every day, and their experiences are such as we have all shared. But in several of her stories, Paramita creates a world that transcends social reality. She says, 'Creativity is often a struggle against social realism.'[3]

The stories in the present collection have been selected by the translator out of a number of collections spanning almost the entire period for which Paramita has been writing, and they reflect the diversity of her creative output. As could be expected, most of the stories are 'gynocentric'. Each story, however, highlights a different facet of the female psyche.

'Colours of Loneliness', our title story, brings us the saga of two childhood friends with contrasting personalities. Maya is shown to be the shyer one, while Veena seems to be the more outgoing one. Maya's life changes as spots begin to appear on her skin, slowly spreading all over her body and face. Her spots become the symbol for loneliness, a matter of pity—everyone assumes the worse life for her. Veena on the other hand gets married into a well-to-do family, and things seem to look up for her. Their lives led in different ways; yet each longs for the life the other has. Loneliness is the bottom line for both the women.

Rina, the protagonist of the first story, 'Wild Jasmine', offers perhaps the subtlest (being the most understated) view of the feminine personality. She is an unspoilt child of nature, a wild jasmine, and falls easy prey to the predator Ratan Singh. But she is not a flower that will wilt and droop: one can sense, though this is not explicitly stated, that she

[3] Personal conversation with Paramita Satpathy.

will stand up and fight. There is an element of ambiguity in the personal calamity that is visited on her and transforms her—one is not sure if she has been physically violated or emotionally brutalized.

Where 'Wild Jasmine' is a page torn out of life, 'The Unborn Daughter's Story' is a fable. There is, as has been said earlier, a well-established tradition in Odisha of storytelling from a feminine perspective, and it is to that tradition that this story goes back, together with the stories captioned 'A Fable for the Times' and 'The Elixir of Love'. 'The Nowhere Nest' focuses on the anguish of the daughter who feels dispossessed and banished, while 'The Ultimate Pay-off' shows the brutality of life when a daughter-in-law becomes the ultimate pay-off for her in-laws' greed. 'Her Best Friend Jaya' deals with female sexuality—rather candidly.

Paramita's sympathies are not restricted to members of her own gender. 'Children's Day' deals with the problem of child abuse and pulls no punches! 'The Girl from a Foreign Land' brings forth repressed emotions to the front, while 'A Shadow in the Mirror' focuses on a haunting past. 'Jungle Lore' brings out the insensitivity and barbarity of the domineering male. 'The N-Club' and 'A Real Diamond!' expose the hollowness of contemporary materialistic culture.

This anthology, in English translation, gives readers across the country access to a sensitive yet powerful voice that has already created an imprint on the Odia mind. I am grateful to the translator, Snehaprava Das, for helping to bring Paramita to a wider readership.

Bikram Das

Wild Jasmine

The forest was aflame.

It was the second half of May and the temperature hovered around forty-five degrees Celsius. The sky poured out molten heat. Like a thirst-tormented monster, the sun sucked up life from every living cell, in man, animal, or plant. There was nothing they could do but surrender meekly to the merciless Nature.

The newly constructed road snaked around the mountain; the work was still on at some places. A few villages stretched out along the roadside. Small huts in a row reached into the forest. On their walls, made of dried-up branches and clay, rested low, sloping thatched roofs. A few had tin or asbestos roofs. Halfway down the looping road stood an asbestos-roofed concrete house with four or five rooms, which served as the *anganwadi* as well as primary school. It was also used sometimes in the evenings for literacy programmes for the elderly.

Most children had stopped coming and the primary school was closed for the summer. But where were the children who used to come to the anganwadi? The heat must be keeping them away, Rina guessed. They should have been there at least for their midday meal. The cooking gas had run out four or five days ago and no refills were to be had in the village. The erratic supply of electricity had broken down completely and no one could tell when it would be restored. Cooking over a wood fire in that heat would mean getting oneself roasted. The house turned into a furnace as heat came streaming down the asbestos roof. There was no respite either inside or outside the house. Rina kept moving in and out, splashing her face from time to time with the water stored in an earthen container.

The sound of a motorbike was heard outside. Who could it be, Rina wondered. Nobody was expected at that hour. It couldn't be her brother Tuku. He had gone out at daybreak to attend some meeting, somewhere inside the forest. It was, he had said, an important meeting and workers from all corners of the state would be coming. Tuku would be late: it might be evening or even night by the time he returned. Rina kept the front door open on account of the heat. She walked out of the courtyard and tried to look out through the open door, stretching forward.

A motorcycle with two men astride it had pulled up outside the house. Their eyes strayed across the open door. Should Rina come out and ask them what they wanted? Perhaps they were new here and wanted to ask the name of the village or the place that the road led to; or maybe they wanted to know something about the construction sites. It was not unusual; many people came inquiring. But it was the timing that troubled Rina. Two strangers arriving during the scorching and deserted afternoon was not usual. Rabi Jani, the tribal domestic help at the anganwadi, had not yet come. She had kept some *pakhala* for him in a bowl and covered it up. Rina waited for the two men to leave. But they did not go; nor did they get off the bike. There was no one in the vicinity she could call in case she needed help. Rina was feeling ill at ease. It might be wiser to shut the door quickly.

'Can we get some water to drink?'

Rina heard one of them speak as she was about to close the door. She stopped abruptly and looked up at the riders. Two young men, in T-shirts and trousers, were looking at her expectantly. Both wore caps. Perhaps they were on their way to attend to some work but the heat and thirst had made them stop, Rina thought. They dismounted and, after parking the bike, moved a few steps towards her. She was a little frightened; should she slam the door in their faces? But they appeared visibly tormented by thirst and heat. They had probably travelled a long distance. They might be in genuine need of water.

'It is so hot here; our throats are parched. There is no shed nearby where we could take shelter for a while,' the man who had been driving the bike said, looking at Rina, and sat down on the veranda without waiting for her to say something. The other man stood on the road, looking ahead. She paused for a moment—the two men were not looking at her. She drew a breath of relief and went inside without a word. She returned in a minute carrying two metal tumblers filled with cool water from the earthen pitcher. The two men almost snatched the tumblers out of her hands and gulped the water down.

'Some more!'

Rina could read the urgency in the man's voice even though neither of them looked at her directly. This time too, she went back without answering, taking the empty glasses and came back after filling them with water. But this time, while returning the empty glasses, the man who had been riding pillion gave her a plastic bottle.

'Can you please fill this bottle?' he said politely.

Rina could not refuse, but she was worried within. Who are these men? Did they know that she was all alone there? What if they followed her into the house?

But none of her misgivings came true. She filled the bottle and handed it back to the man.

'Many thanks,' the man who had been driving the bike said, smiling gratefully at her, and started the engine. Rina went inside, closed the door with one quick movement, and stood leaning against it. 'Many thanks', she muttered to herself and smiled. She was soaked in perspiration. It was unusual to sweat so much in that dry scorching heat.

Rabi Jani's main task was to get firewood and two pitchers of drinking water for the anganwadi. He also filled the earthen vessel in the courtyard with water for washing and cleaning. Besides, when the school was open and more water was needed for the children, he filled a few plastic buckets for their use. Rina had to humour him to get him to do all these chores. Rabi Jani was given a midday meal at the anganwadi in return for the work. But that day, he had not shown up at all. Rina was left to herself in the lonely, blazing afternoon.

෴

It was late afternoon. Rina cycled to the market for some groceries, leaving Rabi Jani in charge of the house. There was no news of Tuku. He had said he would come back by evening,

or at night if he was delayed. He had taken Rina's mobile
phone with him. Of course, a mobile phone was not of much
use in these parts: most of the time the signal was too weak
or entirely dead. But Tuku had not returned at night. Rina
waited for him until midnight. Night faded into morning, but
he did not return. Nor was there any sign of him at noon.
Where was he? Rina was worried. Tuku had been wandering
over the countryside, God knew where, for the last two or
three months. He had opened an STD booth in the market
down below but it remained closed on most days. Tuku did
not seem to have any interest in the shop. Unmindfully,
Rina rolled her bicycle down the winding road. The beep of
a motorcycle horn behind her made her swerve to the left.
The motorcycle stopped by her side. Rina looked at the rider.
It was the man who had come to the anganwadi yesterday
asking for water. But he was alone now; his friend was not
with him.

'Those two glasses of water saved our lives yesterday,' he
said. 'I'm glad I got another chance to say thank you.'

Rina got off the bicycle and smiled at the man.

'Is it always this hot here?' the man said in a low voice, as
if speaking to himself. Rina did not reply.

'Do you belong to this village?' he asked again, looking at
Rina.

She shook her head. 'I work in the anganwadi and stay
there. My home is in a village near Kesinga,' she said casually.

'I've come here for the first time,' the man said. 'I've been
moving from place to place in this heat for the last seven or
eight days, supervising the road construction.'

Rina did not react to this.

'My name is Ratan Singh. I am from Chandikhol. Do you know the place?'

Rina shook her head.

'Were you going somewhere in particular or just roaming around?'

'I was going to the market,' she answered.

'I'm going there too,' the man said. There was a note of eagerness in his voice.

Rina got on to her bicycle.

'Will I get some water the next time I come to your anganwadi?' he asked, gazing intently at Rina. She did not say anything but a soft smile flickered across her face.

'Well, thanks again,' he said and started the motorbike.

It was dark by the time Rina returned from the market. From a distance, she saw Tuku sitting on the veranda.

'Where've you been? There was no news of you,' Rina said with anxiety in her voice.

'I'll tell you everything, didi. Give me something to eat first. Is there any pakhala left?'

Rina stood the bicycle against the wall and hurried inside carrying the groceries. She came out soon with a bowl of pakhala and a plate of fried potatoes. She put the food before Tuku and sat by him, peeling an onion.

'What do these people think? Can they crush us under their feet? Reduce us to dust? They want to build their factories on our land and suck away our blood.' Tuku muttered, looking into the darkness, as if thinking aloud. He had forgotten his sister sitting near him. His hand had stopped in the act of raising food to his mouth. His mind seemed to be elsewhere and he appeared to have been gripped by some deep, overwhelming passion.

'Stop blabbering!' Rina said. 'You have been wandering about for the last two days. You haven't even eaten in these two days. Finish your pakhala first.'

Her voice broke the spell.

'We shall fight, didi. We'll not let them move even a step as long as we live; we will fight to the last drop of blood in our bodies. And after that, *you*, didi, and all the tribal women and girls must take the lead.' Tuku said, still looking into the darkness, as if he was making a prophecy.

Rina kept quiet. They sat there in silence for a few minutes. Tuku lifted the rice from the bowl to his mouth absent-mindedly. Rina looked at the bowl and went inside to get some more rice for him.

'What are these boys up to?' she wondered. Tuku never said anything clearly. He just kept mumbling in broken sentences. They were conducting meetings in unknown villages, somewhere deep inside the forest. He told her just that much, nothing more, although she tried to pry more out of him. This time, he had stayed away for two days without any information. Rina felt a shudder of fear. She let out a deep breath and came back carrying some more rice in a small bowl.

Rina had hoped that the heat would come down a little in the next two days, but instead, the temperature went up. Tuku had gone away somewhere early in the morning. He had been in a great hurry. Rina had mashed some soaked *chooda* for him. But despite all her persuasion, Tuku went away without taking any food. The anganwadi children had not shown up either. Probably no child will come today as well, Rina thought.

The sound of a motorbike was heard outside. Rina came out of the house. It was as if she had been waiting for someone. It was the same young man, Ratan Singh—but he was alone that day.

'I'm really very thirsty today. Can I have two glasses of that refreshing water?' he said, getting off the bike and moving towards the house.

A smile appeared on Rina's face; she went into the house and came back carrying two glasses of water, one in each hand.

'Do you have electricity here?' Ratan Singh asked as he sat down on the veranda.

'Yes, but we've had no power for the last four days. There is a table fan but it is of no use without electricity.'

'There was no storm or rain recently—then why the power failure?' Ratan Singh asked, looking at her.

'Who knows? Perhaps the wires melted in this heat. It's nothing new. The electricity goes away regularly for ten or fifteen days every month.'

'There is no one here to talk to, not even down there in the market,' Ratan Singh said as Rina picked up the empty glasses. 'Do your parents live here? I think there is a school here as well?'

'No, only my younger brother lives with me. There *is* a school but it is closed for the summer vacation,' Rina answered.

'Do the children come regularly? Is there a teacher?'

'Only a few come. They used to come in larger numbers when midday meals were provided, but now, they come only when they feel like it. A teacher has been appointed but he's just as irregular as the children.'

'What about your brother? What does he do for a living? Is he educated?'

'Not much. He passed matriculation but we couldn't afford to send him to school after that. He has opened an STD booth in the market and is planning to stock provisions and a few other things.' She tried to sound carefree but her voice was gloomy.

'Well, I must leave now. Thank you.' Ratan Singh walked back to the motorbike. He looked at Rina, smiled, and started the bike. 'I shall come tomorrow.' Rina could not understand if it was a promise or a proposition. Her face reddened.

Next afternoon, Rina was feeling a bit restless. She walked to and from the front yard of the house many times, expecting Ratan Singh at any moment. Why should he want to come, she asked herself. What would she say to him if he did come? An unidentifiable disquiet had taken possession of her. But Ratan Singh did not come. Noon passed. The sun blazed down. Rina rinsed her face and hands, spread a straw mat on the floor, and lay down. Suddenly, the sound of the motorcycle reached her ears. She got up hurriedly and rushed out.

'I'm not just thirsty today but hungry too. I could do with some tea,' Ratan Singh said softly to Rina and smiled.

A smile touched Rina's lips and lit up her face.

'Isn't your brother home? I thought I could meet him if I came in the late afternoon,' Ratan Singh said.

'No, he may be at his booth.'

'All right, I'll wait here for the tea.' He sat down on the veranda.

'There's no milk,' Rina said, her face flushed with embarrassment.

'Do you have tea leaves and sugar?' Ratan Singh asked. She nodded. 'Black tea will do.' He flicked a smile at her and Rina disappeared into the house.

There was no gas. She would have to use dry leaves to start a fire and prepare tea, Rina thought bitterly. But at last, the tea was ready. Rina came out carrying a cup of tea and four biscuits on a plastic plate.

'It took you a long time!' he said.

'There's no gas,' Rina smiled awkwardly and turned to go inside. 'I'll get a glass of water.'

'Come, sit here,' Ratan Singh said.

Rina put the glass down near him but did not sit down.

'It won't be like this much longer in this village,' he said. 'Life will change. You will be able to get gas easily and there won't be power failures. There will be a bigger market and more shops. Better schools, may be a college as well, and a hospital and doctors. The look of this place will change totally.' Ratan Singh did not look straight at Rina while saying all this although he sat facing her.

Rina stood there silently, listening to him.

'Do you know what we are doing here? We are constructing a road that will connect this mountain to the larger one behind—a real wide concrete road on which two large vehicles can move side by side comfortably, not like the narrow one you have now.' The note of assurance in his voice had remained unchanged.

'Aren't they going to blast the mountain and dig mines there?' Rina returned accusingly.

'Well, not exactly. But whatever will be done will be for the good of everybody. All the people living in these villages will prosper from the project,' he said calmly.

'How will they be better off?'

'They will get jobs. Not just that—they will get cash, good clothes to wear. They will live like real human beings. They will become civilized.' Ratan Singh went on.

'What do you mean by "real human beings"?' Rina asked acidly. 'They are as much human as those you call "civilized". They feel pleasure and pain just the same way as the others; summer and winter have the same effect on them. The only difference is that they are poor. But they do not feel deprived in any way. Have they ever begged for your charity?' Rina grew excited.

'But you must admit that they have benefited from the government's programmes. There are schools for their children, borewells to provide drinking water. Electricity has come to many villages. Medicines have become available. Can you deny it?' Ratan Singh asked.

'No, I admit there are some changes, but most of it is just eyewash. The less said about the government schools, the better. As for healthcare, there is neither a doctor nor medicines in the village dispensary. The power supply is down more often than not.' Rina sounded bitter.

Rabi Jani arrived with buckets full of water hanging at each end of a bamboo pole balanced on his shoulder. He paused a little at the doorstep and glanced first at Ratan Singh and then at Rina. He went inside to keep the buckets and came out. Without saying anything to Rina, he walked away and soon disappeared in the dusk.

'Shall we go for a walk?' Ratan Singh asked Rina in a tender voice. 'Will you show me around the village?'

Rina waited for a moment, turned, and closed the door from outside and fastened it with a chain. She stepped into her slippers and came down the two steps onto the road. They walked along the track that passed by the left of the anganwadi. There were no other houses in the neighbourhood. The huts in these hillside villages were built one behind another in a row, at a little distance from each other. One village was at least ten or twelve kilometres away from the next.

'Whatever you may say, life is hard for the people here. Don't you think they deserve a few modern comforts?' Ratan's tone was calm.

'But why should they have to give up their traditional ways for the sake of these modern comforts? Would *your* people be prepared to do it?' Rina's words erupted suddenly, as though they had been kept suppressed somewhere inside her for a long, long time. 'Can you claim that the life you live is the best?' Rina went on. 'These innocent people mind their own business; they never hurt anyone or try to grab another's share. In what way are they inferior?'

'You are becoming too serious; that was not what I meant,' said Ratan. 'Whatever the government is doing is for their good. They may not understand this now, but they will surely realize it later. I agree that they have been living a life of their own, but trust me, no one intends them any harm,' Ratan Singh pleaded.

They were both silent for a few moments. 'Perhaps it would be a good idea to wash them clean, dress them up in expensive clothes, and put them in cages, like animals in a zoo, so that the rich people from the city could come and gaze at them,' Rina retorted sardonically.

'You really care about them, don't you?' Ratan Singh's voice was placating.

'I have been living among them for the last two years, babu. Believe me, you cannot find such peace anywhere else.' Rina's voice was as calm as Ratan's.

'Don't call me babu—my name is Ratan.'

They walked on in silence. The sun had set. A film of darkness was beginning to spread across the sky. A soft cool breeze blew through the trees, relieving the heat.

'What a sweet smell! What is it?' Ratan Singh stopped and looked around to trace the source of the fragrance.

'Look at that tree on your left, it is a wild fig tree. What you are getting is the smell of its ripe fruits.' Abruptly, Rina stopped. 'Can you recognize this other smell?' She looked at Ratan Singh. 'It is the fragrance of the wild jasmine.' She picked a bunch of soft white flowers from a shrub nearby and handed it to Ratan Singh.

'Wild jasmine.' Ratan Singh's hand touched Rina's, holding the bunch of flowers. Neither said a word. The forest was so unusually quiet that even the sound of a leaf being blown away by the wind could have been heard. Rina held her head lowered.

'Why is it that all white flowers bloom only in the night?' she murmured, looking at the ground.

'All white flowers!' Ratan Singh said gently. He cupped her face in his hands and lifted it close to his own. Their lips met.

'I shall come tomorrow at this time. I am building a small two-roomed house for myself a little above the market, two or three kilometres away. The house that I have rented, in the market place, is too far away from the work site. When the new house is built, I shall take you there.'

They walked back along the path, hand in hand.

ᏬᏬ

Rina was surprised to find Ratan Singh in front of her house so early that morning. They usually met in the evenings. Only last evening, they had spent quite some time in each other's company in Ratan's newly constructed house. What could have been so urgent as to bring him here early in the morning?

Fortunately, Tuku was away. He had left at about noon yesterday and not returned. She walked up to Ratan Singh. He sat astride his bike. He looked flustered; his hair was dishevelled and his eyes were red and swollen. An unknown fear seized her. What could have happened?

'Where is Tuku? Is he at home?' Ratan Singh asked awkwardly.

'I don't know; he could be in his booth in the market,' she replied

'When did he go?' His voice sounded distant, as though he was a stranger.

'Early this morning,' Rina replied, her voice quivering. 'Why? What is the matter?'

'Someone murdered Pradip last night. His dead body was found lying in the market early this morning. He was stabbed in the stomach. The police are searching for the killer; he cannot get away.'

Rina stood rooted to the ground. She had seen Pradip for
the first time when he came to her house with Ratan Singh
on his motorbike, asking for water. Later, she had met him
a few more times at Ratan's new house. Who could have
killed him?

'I must leave now,' Ratan said. 'We shall talk later.' He
started the motorcycle and rode away. Rina stood still on the
veranda, leaning against the wall. Her mind was in turmoil.
Who could possibly have murdered the man? Where had Tuku
gone since yesterday? She had lied to Ratan. Had Tuku been
responsible? No, never; her brother could go to any length, but
murder...? Rina knew how tender his heart was. Last year, the
gentlemen who came to inspect the school had wanted to go
rabbit hunting. But Tuku had prevented him: 'I don't like any
kind of hunting!' he had declared firmly. Rina remembered
how stubborn her brother was. Rina was afraid she would
be dismissed from her job at the anganwadi, but fortunately,
nothing had happened.

'Why are you meeting that contractor so often?' Tuku had
asked her some time back.

'No, we just see each other occasionally. There's nothing to
it,' Rina had replied evasively.

'Be careful, didi; these are not good people. They have come
here from the city with a purpose—to blast the hills and rob
the poor tribal people of their land and their homes. We should
have nothing to do with them,' Tuku said grimly.

Rina had no answer. What could she have said to her
younger brother? As it was, he was away most of the time. She
could not tell him that she was in love with Ratan Singh, that
they had decided to get married. She couldn't tell him what

she thought of Ratan—that he was not an evil character, as Tuku believed, but a compassionate man, full of sympathy for tribal people. She would talk to her brother one of those days and try to explain things to him, but with this sudden turn of events, all her planning had gone haywire.

It was evening; Tuku did not come back. Rina waited for him with bated breath. Night came and departed. It was another day. There was no sign of Tuku—not that day, nor the next. Four days passed but Tuku did not return. On the fifth night, there was a soft knock on the door. Rina was jolted out of sleep; her body was trembling in fear.

'Didi, open the door.' Tuku's voice came from the other side of the door. Rina jerked the door open. Tuku and three or four other boys stood outside.

'Is there something to eat?' he asked urgently.

Rina had not cooked. She was not able to think properly. She rushed into the kitchen, soaked some chooda in a bowl of water, strained out the water, and, after adding some sugar to it, handed the bowl to Tuku and his friends. Then she slumped on the floor, worn out.

'Listen, didi, the police are after us. But we haven't killed that man. You must trust me, didi, some others murdered him and are trying to frame us.' Tuku was gasping for breath. Rina's gaze travelled to the pistol and knives that they had put down on the floor. She was startled, as if she had seen a snake.

'These are nothing, didi, just for self-defence. We are wandering here and there, hiding ourselves from the police. We are compelled to keep these things, just in case. Do you have some money?' Tuku asked impatiently.

Rina hurried towards her tin box and took out all the money from it, including the small coins. She counted the money— 556 rupees in all—and handed it over to her brother. Tuku snatched the money from her hand. He and the others went out through the back door and disappeared into the darkness. Rina felt her legs weakening and sat down at the very place where she had been standing. She sat huddled up through the rest of the night. When it was daylight, she got up somehow and attended to the domestic chores with much effort. A few anganwadi children had turned up; she gave them some singing practice. She thought she would cook for them but she felt so disturbed that she had to abandon the idea. She gave each of them a couple of biscuits and sent them back. Rabi Jani came in the afternoon. 'Shall I get water?' he asked Rina.

'Have you seen Ratan Singh?' Rina asked him and he shook his head.

She secured the front door and came out onto the road soon after Rabi Jani left. She began walking in the direction of Ratan Singh's house, hoping that Ratan Singh would come riding his motorbike at any moment. But the road was completely deserted. She trudged on. By the time she reached Ratan Singh's house, about three kilometres away, she was out of breath. It was quite late in the evening. To her disappointment, both the rooms were locked from the outside. She sat down for a while on the veranda to rest her legs. There was not a soul around, nor was there any chance of getting a little water to wet her parched throat. She half ran, half walked back to the anganwadi. She spent a sleepless night, sick with worry. In the morning, she decided that she must find Ratan Singh at any cost. If she did not find him in his house, she would go down to the market and look for him in his usual haunts. 'I must, by any means, make him meet Tuku, explain everything, and remove the suspicion and ill feeling they have for each other,' she kept saying to herself all day, as if reciting a litany.

Rina moved in and out of the house gripped with anxiety, waiting for the sun to set. She did not have the patience to wait for dusk: she took out her bicycle, locked the door, and rode away. It would take her some time to reach Ratan Singh's house, riding uphill along that winding road.

At a little distance from the house, Rina hid her bicycle behind some wild bushes by the roadside and soft-footedly walked down the road towards the back door of the house to avoid being seen by any passer-by. The back door was open. Rina could see a big car parked outside the house. Perhaps Ratan Singh had company. She usually came to this house only if Ratan Singh asked her to, because most of the time, he was out or with friends.

Rina hesitated a little. Should she go in? Most probably there were others in the house along with Ratan Singh. It would not be wise to go inside. Maybe she should call him out.

Still undecided, Rina moved towards the house, a step at a time. Instead of entering through the back door, she took a turn to the left and stood below the window. Standing on tip-toe, she stretched forward a little and tried to peep through the window. The sound of laughter floated out through the room. Rina waited a while, hoping to meet the boy who cooked for Ratan.

'These tribal people are so simple that they will never suspect anything, even if someone cuts their feet away under them,' Rina heard someone say. It was Ratan Singh's voice.

'But those boys are really smart. It was they who killed Pradip,' someone else remarked.

'Don't worry, we'll get them soon. I have managed to trap their leader's sister and we will come to know of their whereabouts from her.' It was Ratan Singh again.

Rina could not believe her ears; could this be Ratan Singh speaking?

'You are an expert at trapping girls!' a voice said admiringly. 'Otherwise, life would be boring in a place like this. What is she like?'

'A real masala dish! Wait until you get a taste!' Ratan Singh said. A burst of vulgar, raucous laughter followed.

Rina turned to stone. Her head whirled. She was not able to decide whether she should go in and reveal her presence or return unnoticed.

'But aren't you afraid of AIDS, brother? We need to take precautions.'

'Yes, you must be careful. Anyway, the road will be built in a few months and then we can all go home. Why bother?'

'But Pradip's death must be avenged.'

Without turning, Rina moved back carefully, step by step. The jungle was so dangerously quiet that the sound of a foot treading on a dry leaf could have been heard.

There was no time to take the bicycle out of the place where she had hidden it. She ran blindly through the forest, trampling the wild bushes and undergrowth, getting bruised and scratched by the spiky creepers that were entangled with one another. She seemed to be running for her life, as though the men in the room were chasing her.

More surprise awaited her at the anganwadi. The front door was open. A friend of Tuku's was pacing about in front of the house; perhaps he kept vigil over the place. He stopped when he saw Rina. Without a word, she half walked and half ran into the house. In a corner of the veranda sat Tuku and some of his friends. Rina did not wait to look at them properly, nor did she say anything to Tuku. She ran straight into her room.

The forty-watt bulb in her room gave out a very dim light because of the low voltage. Rina stood before the small mirror hanging on the wall. She was startled at the sight of her reflection.

'Do you know, didi? The fellow that murdered that contractor has been caught this afternoon. There is a rumour that the killer belonged to a rival group,' Tuku said standing at the door; there was eagerness and relief in his voice.

Rina turned and stood facing her brother. Tuku stopped short. Even in that dim light, he could see the scratches on his sister's face; he could see the thin line of blood that trickled down her cheek. She had not worn a dupatta over her dress. A portion of the left sleeve of her kameez was torn and hung awkwardly. Tuku stood still as a statue for an instant.

'Didi, what happened? Who has done this? Tell me!' The grimness in Tuku's voice was frightening.

Rina stood woodenly, holding her head down. Tears had begun to well up in her eyes.

'Didi, I am asking you something!' Tuku roared. His friends sitting on the veranda heard him and came there. Standing behind him, they tried to peep through the door.

'It was he—that contractor babu and his friends,' Rina's tone was calm and clear. She fixed her eyes on Tuku's face.

She did not blink even once while she said this although tears ran down her eyes.

'Where are they?'

'In his house.'

Rina shifted her gaze towards Tuku's friends standing behind him.

Without uttering a word, Tuku turned and stormed out of the room. His friends followed him. Moving with the speed of lightning, they reached the other end of the veranda and the clash of metal on metal was heard. Rina tried to see—there were knives and other weapons in their hands that glittered in the dim light. Tuku and his six friends leaped away like wild animals and melted into the darkness in an instant.

Rina stood still at the threshold holding the door in both hands and kept looking into the darkness. Tears trickled down her eyes.

The Unborn Daughter's Story

The case was being heard in the family court.

There were not many people in the courtroom. A few briefless lawyers loitered in the corridor; some sat on the spectators' bench at the rear, talking excitedly among themselves. Snigdha and her parents sat in silence. Amar and Dinesh, friends of Pradeep, sat at a distance from them, watching the scene with interest.

The courtroom was not very large. Pradeep stood facing his advocate.

'The case appears to be complicated,' the lawyer said. 'This is no ordinary case of legal separation. We will need your full cooperation—is that clear?'

'Yes, sir,' Pradeep said.

'You think that your wife has become mentally deranged. Am I right?'

'Yes, sir.'

'But Dr Chopra, the psychiatrist who examined her, reports that he found nothing abnormal in her behaviour.'

'That's true, sir, but he also says that no one in her right mind would do what she did.'

'All right,' the lawyer said. 'Let me ask you something else. How long have you been married?'

'Nearly two years. We were married on 2 January 1984.'

'Did you know each other before marriage?'

'Yes.'

'For how long?'

'A year or so,' Pradeep said. 'Her elder brother, Atanu, was my classmate. We were in the same college at Rourkela. I had been to their home once during a vacation and met her there. Slowly, we came to like each other....' Pradeep paused, feeling a little embarrassed.

'Now, let me ask you something personal. What was your conjugal life like?'

Pradeep looked around before answering, feeling even more embarrassed.

'Fine,' he said.

'Did you ever have any serious differences of opinion?'

'Not that I can remember.'

'When did this incident occur?'

'Nearly six months ago.'

'Did your wife try to explain her behaviour to you?'

'Yes, sir. She tried to convince me that what she had done was out of some temporary aberration. You might have formed a similar opinion yourself.'

'So, now you want a divorce from your wife on the ground that she has lost her mental balance, right?' the advocate asked, ignoring Pradeep's remark.

He turned to face the judge and said, 'Your Honour, I must at this stage stress the point that Dr Chopra's report says nothing about any noticeable symptoms of mental disorder in Mrs Mishra. That's all for now.'

The court room was abuzz with hushed, excited whispers.

Snigdha turned slightly in her seat to look around. Her husband and his two friends sat with their back turned to her. They looked relaxed, as if nothing serious had happened. Her parents-in-law had not come to the court. They would not have been comfortable watching the proceedings. From the corner of her eye, she stole a glance at her parents. Her mother's face looked unusually pale, as if someone had drained all the blood out of it. Her father sat stiffly in a chair, looking as if he had been chained to it. He seemed ready to run away, given the slightest opportunity. The shadow of humiliation had darkened his otherwise pleasant face. The court might not issue the final order today—that would mean another hearing and another day of agony!

'Madam, I'm Advocate Choudhury,' a voice said close to her.

Snigdha sat up to look at the man who had spoken to her.

'You don't know me personally but I have heard the entire history of the case from your father. I visited your place a couple of times but unfortunately you were out on both occasions. I wish we could have discussed this case before coming to court—but never mind! I'm sure we won't have to appeal in the high court. The judge will pass the order for your legal separation today; there won't be any problem on that account. But we shall not accept the allegation of insanity brought against you. There is no valid evidence to prove it. Besides, the doctor did not mention any such thing in his report, so you needn't worry. Oh, here comes Dr Behera! We can begin now,' Advocate Choudhury said as he strode away briskly to his table.

'Hello, Snigdha! Sorry I'm a little late,' Dr Behera said apologetically.

'It's all right,' Snigdha said and moved to a side of the bench, making room for Dr Behera. 'Please have a seat,' she said. But her husband's advocate called Dr Behera. 'Dr Behera, could you kindly come here, please?'

Dr Behera took her seat across the table and swore an oath on the Holy Gita. She adjusted her sari across her shoulder, took out a handkerchief from her handbag, and wiped her face.

'Do you know Mrs Mishra?' the advocate asked.

'Yes, we were in college at the same time while doing the Intermediate Science course, although she was a year my junior. We still meet often as we live in the same town.'

'You performed the abortion. How old was the foetus at the time the pregnancy was terminated?'

'About ten weeks.'

'Why did she want an abortion? Did she tell you?' the advocate carried on with his questioning.

'She told me that it was too early for her to have a baby and she wasn't mentally prepared. I asked if her husband felt the same way. I said he should have been there with her to lend her support but she said that Pradeep, her husband, was out of town on an official tour and wouldn't be back for ten or twelve days. She assured me that he shared her feeling. I've known Snigdha for quite a long time and had no reason to doubt what she told me.'

'Very well,' the advocate said and changed the line of questioning. 'Have you ever come across such a case before, Dr Behera?' he asked.

Dr Behera shook her head. 'No.'

'Do you think the reason that Mrs Mishra gave for wanting an abortion could be true?'

'I have no idea.'

'Still, as a doctor, have you ever heard or read about a case such as this?' the advocate persisted.

'No, not until now,' Dr Behera answered briefly.

'Could this have been the result of some psychological disorder in Mrs Mishra? What is your opinion?' Pradeep's advocate asked persuasively.

'How can I answer that?' Dr Behera replied. 'I am a gynaecologist, not a psychiatrist.'

'Very well,' Pradeep's advocate said. 'Your turn, Mr Choudhury,' he said and withdrew.

Advocate Choudhury walked up to Dr Behera.

'Termination of pregnancy is no longer illegal,' he said. He made it sound like a question and not a statement.

'That is correct, yes,' Dr Behera replied.

'You started your medical practice only recently, Dr Behera, and so such a case has not come your way yet. But could you rule out the possibility of such an incident happening in future?'

'I have absolutely no idea, to be honest,' Dr Behera said truthfully. 'Such an incident had not come to my notice before. It will be the first of its kind, if we accept it as authentic.'

'Have you ever noticed any temporary neurotic disorder in Mrs Mishra?'

'I examined her thoroughly soon after the incident. There was absolutely no such symptom. We have known each other for a long time, as I have already stated, but I have never seen her behaving abnormally at any time,' Dr Behera said emphatically.

'One last question, Dr Behera. Would you have believed her if she had told you the real reason for which she wanted her pregnancy terminated?'

'Perhaps not. I would have called her husband and sought his opinion.'

'You may go now,' the lawyer said to Dr Behera. He turned to face the judge. 'Your Honour! Mrs Mishra aborted her pregnancy without the knowledge of her husband. That may be a valid enough reason for a separation. But the allegation of insanity brought against Mrs Mishra has not been substantiated and must be withdrawn. Two doctors have examined her and both have declared her normal. It leaves no room for doubt regarding Mrs Mishra's sanity. And, as regards the unusual incident that happened, according to her, why should we be so biased as to reject its possibility?'

There were suppressed giggles from someone at the back.

'Now, Mrs Mishra, would you please come here?' Pradeep's advocate said to Snigdha.

Snigdha took her seat and swore to speak the truth, the whole truth, and nothing but the truth.

'Mrs Mishra, do you have a normal relationship with your husband?'

'He is a good man,' Snigdha said and looked at Pradeep. Pradeep averted his eyes, as if determined not to look at his wife.

'What was your reaction when you realized you were pregnant?'

'I was elated. My mother-in-law had guessed it before I told her and had disclosed it to Pradeep. Everyone was so happy. It was almost like a festive occasion at home. I wrote a letter to my mother that very night!' There was an unusual gleam on her face as she narrated the incident.

'Then why didn't you let Mr Mishra know when you decided on an abortion?'

'He wouldn't have agreed.'

'You should have taken his consent. After all, he was the father.'

'I had no alternative,' Snigdha replied. Her voice was firm and steady.

She looked at her parents. They sat with their gaze fixed on the floor as though they were reading something written on it.

'Your husband has told the court that you are having hallucinations. He complains that you have developed insanity. Will you tell the court about the incident that has led him to form this opinion?'

'I have already told Pradeep.'

'This court would want to hear it from you first hand.'

Snigdha looked around the courtroom before speaking. 'It happened on 5 June last year. My mother-in-law was away at her daughter's. Pradeep, my husband, had a dinner programme at his club that night. There was no one else at home except for me and my father-in-law. We had a light dinner. I was feeling sleepy. I asked our servant to open the front door for my husband when he returned and went to bed. Soon I was fast asleep.

'Suddenly, in the middle of the night, I heard a voice, a baby's voice. "Maa," it called out. I was startled out of my sleep. It was half past one in the morning. No sound was heard except the gentle snoring of Pradeep.'

'Wait,' the advocate cut in. 'How did you know it was half past one?'

'I looked at the small clock on the bedside table.'

'Tell us what happened after that.'

'It was a full moon night. The window facing the bed had been kept open to let the cool breeze in. The room was bathed in soft moonlight entering through the window. "Maa, Maa," the voice called again. Puzzled out of my wits, I sat up in bed to find the baby that was calling out to its mother at this hour of the night! Everything could be seen clearly in the moonlight. There was no one in the room except Pradeep and me.

'*Then I knew!*

'The voice was coming from within me! I felt terrified! Someone inside me was speaking—a soft, misty voice. The life that I bore inside me had been transformed into a voice.

'*My daughter!*

'I knew that my daughter was speaking from inside my body.'

'How could you be so sure that it was your daughter?' Pradeep's advocate interrupted her. 'How could you be so sure of the child's gender?'

'Of course I knew!' Snigdha said loudly. 'It *was* my daughter. There was no mistaking it. A voice so soft, so heavy with emotion, can only belong to a girl. I was feeling dazed at the eeriness of what was happening. The voice begged me, "Maa, please do not bring me to this earth. Do not let me get caught up in this cruel world and bleed to death at every moment of my existence".'

Snigdha paused for breath. Beads of sweat shone on her forehead.

'Then I saw her,' she went on. 'She came floating on the soft moonlight that streamed in through the window. "Tell me, maa," she said, "is there any space on this earth where I and girls like me can find a place to stand?" What a pathetic appeal her voice held! Tears rolled down my eyes. Everything looked so hazy and blurred. The room, its walls, the bed, nothing was there any longer. Even Pradeep was nowhere in sight. A little girl stood before me. I could not see her clearly but I had no doubt that she was my daughter. No longer able to contain my patience, I stretched out my arms to her. I was desperate to see her face, her smile, to hold her close to my heart. I wanted to kiss all over her tiny face and body. Everything that my fancy had conjured up since the day I first knew about my pregnancy crowded back to my mind at once. But, I wondered, why is she telling me such unhappy things? "Come, my darling, come to me," I said loudly, leaning towards her, my arms outstretched.

'She didn't move. She said nothing. The moonlight bathed her in a stream of liquid silver. In that silver glow, I saw....' Snigdha paused again. Her voice faltered, and her entire body began to tremble.

'Please, carry on, Mrs Mishra,' the advocate prodded her. 'What was it you saw?'

'I saw tears streaming down my daughter's eyes. She was trying to reach out to me but she could not lift her hands. Her lips quivered. Maybe she wanted to say something to me, but no words escaped her lips. Instead, rivulets of blood ran down from her mouth. As I gaped at her, horror-struck, blood gushed out of her eyes, her nose, her cheeks, her hands and feet. She was drowning in a cascade of blood. I tried to scream, but my voice was choked. I wanted to wake up everyone and tell them about it. But no one was there to listen to me. Slowly, the blood-soaked image of my daughter melted away. I was back in my room, lying in my own bed. Everything was as it had been. Pradeep turned on his side. I was soaked in perspiration. I thought I should wake my husband up and tell him everything, but I decided against it. I knew he would dismiss it as a bad dream and ask me to go back to sleep. So I lay there quietly, propped up against the pillow, still feeling dazed. Pradeep woke up a little later. He drank water from the glass kept on the bedside table and went back to sleep. He did not know that I was awake. It was almost dawn. The air had become cool. In the garden at the back of the house, a cuckoo began to sing. By then, I had made up my mind.'

Snigdha stopped speaking and glanced around. Everyone seemed to be staring at her, their eyes wide in disbelief. A stunned silence hung over the courtroom. Snigdha's parents sat still, hanging their heads even lower. Pradeep and his friends sat in silence, their eyes downcast.

'It means that you knowingly, purposefully took a life. What if she asked you to do the deed? Would you kill your parents if they made a similar appeal?' Pradeep's advocate demanded.

'Never! I would never take a human life. Are you accusing me of murdering my own daughter? Do you know how much I loved her? I told you she was in pain, terrible pain. But I could not do anything to relieve her of the pain. Nobody could help her. Why did she have to suffer so much? Who was responsible? Why couldn't she find even a small space on the earth to put down her tiny, delicate feet? How could I have seen her in such pain? What right did I have to bring her to this earth and fling her into a whirlpool of torture?' She seemed to be talking to herself in a voice that was barely audible. Her eyes were fixed on some invisible thing on the floor as she spoke.

'Nevertheless, what you did is a blot on the sanctity of motherhood,' the advocate who had argued in favour of Pradeep said, letting out a deep sigh.

'I had only tried to understand and respect motherhood,' Snigdha returned solemnly, raising her head to face him.

'I suppose you wouldn't have dared to take this extreme step had abortion not been legalized.' Pradeep's advocate, after much deliberation, had used his last weapon to prop up his client's stand.

'I would have done exactly what I did now, even if we moved a thousand years back in time,' Snigdha replied in a steady voice.

There was a moment of total silence, before the courtroom erupted.

The Elixir of Love

The afternoon was ripe by the time I reached the place.

How many people would even have heard of it, I wondered. But to me, it appeared strangely familiar, as if I had been there before. It was like reliving a forgotten experience.

It was difficult to figure out what made the place feel so unusual. There was something strange about it that I couldn't lay my fingers on. On the surface, everything was normal. Yet a feeling of desolation clung to me as I moved on. No one paid any attention to me; they all looked preoccupied. Each seemed to be absorbed in some solemn task, which they performed with unrelenting commitment. There was no laxity in anybody's efforts to discharge their responsibility. But there was no trace of any emotional involvement in what they were doing. Something was missing. It was not easy to define the experience. Imagine a mother who feeds her baby but does not hold it close to her bosom; a student reading a book without the curiosity to discover its message; a housewife cooking a curry without bothering to taste a drop of the gravy to make sure it has the right amount of salt; a gardener watering a plant with no eagerness to see the flower blooming. The ambience upset me. I decided that this wasn't a place to live in and turned to leave.

'Wait, are you going away?' a voice asked. I was a stranger here. Who would want to speak to me? I looked around. 'You don't seem to like it here. It's because this is your first visit to this place. You'll get used to it.' The man who spoke to me was old and wore a saintly look. He was dressed in white and held a small brass water-pot by its handle.

'Why is everyone here like this?' my voice trembled with emotion as I asked him.

'You find something abnormal about them, do you?'

'Exactly,' I said, encouraged. 'Yogi baba, I am puzzled by their total apathy.'

'They don't have a heart,' the yogi answered flatly.

'No heart!' I was astounded. 'But they are all live human beings, not machines. How can a human being exist without a heart?'

'True. From a clinical point of view, they do have hearts. But the hearts do not have any feeling.'

It sounded ridiculous to me. I managed to stop myself from laughing out loud and asked, 'What does that mean?'

'Listen, my child,' the yogi explained patiently. 'God puts a bright, gold-coloured coating over our hearts when He breathes life into us. The coating is in a fluid state when we are young but it hardens as we grow in years. But there are exceptions: some hearts remain soft forever. Their owners have to face a lot of difficulty because a person with a soft heart is condemned to live under constant stress and spend sleepless nights. To escape this fate, some try to wrench the golden coating out and hide it in a hole under the earth or in the hollow of a tree. Some put it away in a gunny bag and abandon it in the depths of a dense forest; others keep it tied in a bundle, which they throw into a flowing river or toss into burning flames or even fling down from the terrace of a high-rise building. But they are unaware of what they are doing. Ask them and they will feign ignorance. They adopt every possible means to keep it away from their sight.

'Some people of this category have settled here. And that is why it appears strange to you.'

How unfortunate for them, I thought. I reproached myself silently for my earlier reaction.

'Will they remain this way till the end?' I asked.

'Yes. Not just they, but their progeny too will inherit the legacy of apathy. If at all, by the remotest chance, one manages to retain the layer of emotion covering the heart, others will not let him keep it. They will try to tear it off.'

'Isn't there a way out?' I entreated. 'Can't something be done to help them?'

'Not by me—but yes, there *is* a way. If....' The yogi stopped abruptly.

'Please tell me what it is,' I asked impatiently.

'If some woman with a sympathetic heart were to bring a pitcher full of the elixir of love and sprinkle it over these people, they would be transformed into the kind of human beings you would like them to be,' the yogi explained.

'I shall do it!' I said instantly, filled with enthusiasm. 'Just tell me what I have to do.' Suddenly, I was gripped by a frenzy of philanthropy. I was determined to rescue this mass of decaying humanity.

'Are you sure? It will be tough,' the yogi warned me.

'It doesn't matter; I will do it! Give me a chance. Tell me where I can find the elixir,' I begged.

The yogi looked intently at me for a while and his face lit up with a genial smile.

'Fine,' he said, 'You will have to travel a long way to get there. You cannot miss the place; you will recognize it as soon as you see it. Once you reach it, you must collect some of the elixir and return here. I will then begin the work of sprinkling it over these people.' He turned and, opening a big boat-shaped bundle, took something out of it.

'These are some medicinal roots and herbs. Take them; who knows, you may have to face unexpected difficulties. You could get injured, scratched by thorns, or fall into a pit and get hurt. There will be some who will try to rob you of every iota of your energy. If, through God's grace, you do overcome these hurdles, the ordeal will surely wear you out. You have, after all, the tender body of a woman. But never fear. Touch this medicinal root to your body and you will feel as strong as ever.'

'What about *my* heart, yogi baba?' I asked. 'Don't you have something for my heart?' He did not reply but turned again and took out a blue sling bag with a zipper. He pulled open the zipper, put the roots and the pills in it, pulled back the zipper, and slung the bag on my shoulder. The colour of the bag went well with my sari.

My journey into the unknown began.

The first thing that came to view after I had covered a long distance was an ethereal palace. What grandeur it possessed! It seemed to have been filled with all the luxuries of the world. People moved around in dazzling clothes and jewellery and feasted on delicious dishes. The young ones lived exuberant lives. They gladly took me into their group and I, like them, soon learnt to enjoy life to its brim. I didn't have the slightest inclination to leave the place, until I remembered the promise I had made to the yogi. His face, pale with concern, and the trust he had reposed in me began to haunt me, and the next morning, I resumed my journey leaving the beautiful palace and my young companions behind.

Words cannot describe the misery that awaited me thereafter. The path was impassable, filled with potholes and ditches; thorny creepers lay entwined in my path. Each step had to be taken with great caution. There were huge abysses concealed under rocks; one wrong step and a traveller could sink into unknown depths. Swiftly flowing mountain streams appeared here and there, bridged only by slender, frail-looking trunks of palm trees. At times, I had to traverse deep ravines, clinging to a rope that spanned two cliffs. The slightest distraction would have been disastrous. Again and again, I was filled with doubt. Why did I, of all people, have to pursue this perilous path? Why did I volunteer to get the elixir of love for those people?

Somehow, with superhuman effort that I never knew I was capable of, I managed to negotiate those treacherous paths and reached a point where, to my great relief, a river came into view. It was so broad that the other bank couldn't be seen. How was I to cross? But I *had* to go ahead; there could be no turning back. I looked around for some sort of help—either a boat or a boatman—but not a soul was in sight. I walked for some distance along the bank. I saw a raft tied to the trunk of a tree by the riverside. Would it be wise to try to cross the river on this frail raft? But there was no alternative. I clambered on board and unfastened the raft. With a silent prayer, I let it float on the current into the wide expanse of that unknown river. It was more than likely, I thought, that the raft would overturn and I would drown; but if that didn't happen, it was certain to touch land at some point. But the raft continued to float slowly. After a long time, it reached the opposite bank.

A scene that was totally unexpected awaited me. I had reached an enormous plain of ice. Wherever I looked, there was nothing but dazzling, barren ice, devoid of any vegetation. Not an animal or human being was to be seen anywhere. The sun was about to set. The ice floor was bathed in an orange glow. Despite the fear that gripped me, my eyes were glued to the lovely sight. But where, on that frozen plain, was I to find the pot of elixir for which I was searching? The yogi had assured me that the pot would announce itself: I would recognize it the moment it appeared. But my quest seemed hopeless.

Could the yogi have known that my entire life had been a desperate quest for the elixir of love? Did he see that I had been running after it not as much for the people who inhabited that strange land as for my own self?

I was confused. Was there really such a miraculous elixir or was I just chasing a delusion? I had travelled far. I might have come across the pot of elixir but failed to notice it. What if I failed to find it? I had encountered all the dangers of which the yogi had warned me. My body was bruised and battered. But I should have no cause for fear. Every time I suffered a hurt or felt exhausted, I only had to touch my body with the yogi's medicinal herbs, and at once, the pain and exhaustion were gone.

The darkness of night slowly enveloped the snow-shrouded plain. Sleep overcame me.

Early next morning, I was awakened by the chirping of birds. I sat up rubbing my eyes and looked around. But what was this? I couldn't believe my eyes. The snow-covered plain had disappeared, and in its place, there was a beautiful garden. The lush green trees were laden with ripe fruits. There were flowers everywhere. I got up and walked about a little, plucked a few fruits and flowers. It was so peaceful! The experience was out of the world! Was I, I asked myself, in heaven? Soft sunlight sneaked through the thick foliage of tall trees and made patterns on the ground. A little ahead, facing me, was a large cave. Lush, green vines heavy with fragrant pink blossoms hemmed its entrance. The scene seemed to have been painted by the brush of some celestial artist. Cautiously, I walked inside. The interior looked like the foyer of a huge palace. I took a few steps forward. The astonishing sight that greeted my eyes took the breath out of me. In the middle of the polished floor of the cave, there stood a conch-white vessel filled with some fluid substance that gleamed like liquid gold! Lotus petals floated in it. I didn't have to think twice to realize that I had found the magic elixir that I had come all this way in search of. I kept staring at the vessel filled with the shining liquid, amazed. Involuntarily, my hand touched the plastic water bottle that hung from my shoulder. 'I have to collect this priceless liquid in this bottle,' I thought. Feeling proud of my own achievement, I moved slowly towards the vessel. Suddenly, a familiar smell filled the cave. It was a smell, I could recall, that was closely linked to the days of my early youth. This lovely smell, I recognized, had once held my entire being captive during those days. What memories that smell was carrying to me! But suddenly, I was startled by the sound of approaching footsteps.

I turned around.

Oh my God, this is Aditya! Aditya! Here!

I gaped at the figure in front of me in disbelief. He was half concealed behind a film of mist. Slowly, the mist dissolved and I saw him clearly. He looked exactly the way he had looked when I had last seen him. His face was pale and his lips puckered. A few strands of unkempt, wind-blown hair hung over his eyes. He held something in his hand. I looked closely. It was something that had withered in the sun but which, I guessed, must have been fresh once. A few, unintelligible words, which I had deliberately avoided listening to years ago, seemed to have frozen on his bloodless lips. I made an effort to string the indistinct words together into a coherent sentence, but they remained unintelligible. I avoided looking into his eyes but I was certain that his gaze was fixed on me. I should be taking the elixir back with me. Nothing, not even Aditya, should distract me. I focused on the task before me, to fill the large plastic bottle and carry it back to the yogi. I turned my face quickly towards the golden liquid in the vessel.

A sound of something crashing to the ground was heard. I turned on my heels to see what had happened. There was no sign of Aditya. A shadowy figure seemed to be slowly disappearing. What was it that had fallen? There were broken fragments lying scattered on the floor of the cave. My body felt damp, with traces of something wet and sticky. I wiped away a little of that sticky substance with my fingertips.

Blood!

I stared at my fingertips, shaken out of my wits. What had broken? Something Aditya had been carrying?

As I looked on, the liquid in the vessel began to change colour; it became green and then acquired an angry orange hue. Slowly, it turned a deep blood red. The lotus petals turned into black, ugly worms and started to swim madly in that pool of blood.

A shiver ran through me. I began to scream, but no sound came.

Where was Aditya?

'Aditya, please come back. I need you,' I called out at the top of my voice. No one answered. The echoes filled the cave. I ran forward a few steps to look. But there was no one in that cave except me. The fragrance that had drenched the air inside the cave too was gone. A deathly silence prevailed everywhere. Pieces of paper, on which something was written in a neat handwriting in blue ink, flew around blown by the gusts of wind. Slowly, the pieces rose higher and higher and disappeared into the black emptiness.

'Yogi baba!' I called out, kneeling on the floor. 'My mission has failed! Long since, I have lost the ability to fetch the elixir of love.' Tears trickled down my eyes.

'Forgive me, Aditya!' I kept on repeating.

My eyes opened. Bright sunlight entering through the chinks in the window panels showed me I was lying on my bed, in the drab, undistinguished government quarters that I occupied. I could feel tears trailing down the corners of my eyes. Somehow, I didn't have the inclination to wipe them away. The hands of the wall clock showed it was only past eight. As I hurriedly got off the bed, I remembered that it was a Sunday.

The Girl from a Foreign Land

'Sidar, you are wonderful!' a familiar sweet voice wafted in from somewhere.

Siddharth was startled. Where did it come from?

He opened the window, and instantly, a blast of marrow-chilling December wind swished into the room. With the wind drifted in a voice, speaking in endearingly soft and accented English. 'Sidar, you are wonderful!'

Siddharth shut the window.

The faint smell of a familiar perfume filled the room. The memory of what had happened in the last three weeks came back to him vividly.

'What is the name of this perfume?' he had asked.

An amused smile flashed across Sylvia's lips. 'It's called "Dune",' she answered. 'Do you know what "dune" means to me? Vast, thick layers of sand stretching away beyond the range of vision into the Sahara Desert!' She had tried to explain. 'Thin, flimsy curtains of sand floating about in the wind, wrapping themselves around the body. My perfume isn't just a name, it is a concept!'

Siddharth had marvelled at the way she explained it. It was very mature for a girl of Sylvia's age.

Dr Chaddha had prevailed on Siddharth to provide Sylvia temporary accommodation in his house. 'You will have to do this for me, Siddharth,' he had begged. 'Sylvia's father is a close friend of mine. He helped me a lot in my research when I was at Dresden University. I don't have a spare room in my house to accommodate a guest for three weeks. You know that Sheela's school final is just round the corner. I can't think of an alternative. She is only twenty-two or so. It is a question of only a couple of weeks, please don't refuse!'

'But she is a young girl and my wife is away. It wouldn't look nice!' Siddharth protested.

'Please, Siddharth, you are my only hope. She is doing some project on oriental languages. Her father has made me responsible for looking after her during her stay in India. She has been brought up delicately. Her father is afraid our climate and the unfamiliar food could affect her health. Please, Siddharth, you have to help me out!' Dr Chaddha insisted. 'Moreover, Sylvia wants to have the experience of living in an Indian home.' He knew that Siddharth's apartment in Vasant Kunj had two bedrooms, each with an attached bath. There was no way out for Siddharth except to comply. He rang up Minati and told her about the arrangement. She didn't sound happy.

The Lufthansa flight that Sylvia had boarded landed on time. Siddharth and Dr Chaddha were at the airport to receive her. It was past two in the night by the time she came out after going through customs. Siddharth guessed correctly that the girl who was walking briskly towards them, trundling a trolley bag and carrying a rucksack on her back, was Sylvia. She was about five foot five inches tall. Her dark golden tresses were held tightly in a ponytail that came down to her shoulders. There was no doubt that the girl was beautiful. The long journey had not left a trace of weariness on her fresh, lively face. Siddhartha looked away from her. He never liked the way Indian men stare hungrily at the women from foreign countries.

'My dear girl,' Prof Chaddha took her in his arms affectionately. 'How was your flight?' he asked. The girl beamed at him. He introduced Siddharth to her: 'Your host!'

'Glad to meet you,' the girl said in halting English. 'Sylvia,' she said and extended a hand. It was not exactly a handshake. Siddharth's fingers touched Sylvia's lightly. Her hand was cold to his touch. The three of them rode back to Siddharth's apartment in his car. Dr Chaddha showed Sylvia her room. It was unfortunate that Siddharth's wife and son were not there to receive her, Dr Chaddha said. She was expecting their second child and had gone, along with their four-year-old son, to her parents in Odisha for the delivery of the baby, the professor told Sylvia.

'To her parents! But why? Aren't there good hospitals in Delhi?' Sylvia asked, looking directly at Siddharth. The astonishment in her eyes was reflected in her voice too. Siddharth felt embarrassed. He had not expected his German guest, who had known him for just for a few hours, to ask such a personal question.

'They have a four-year-old son and Siddharth thought Minati would be better looked after there, by her mother,' Dr Chaddha explained. Sylvia did not say anything but Siddhartha could see the slightly sceptical look in her eyes. She must be thinking how a man who sends his pregnant wife away to her parents in some far-off place could take care of a guest whom he has known for just a few hours, guessed Siddharth. He felt annoyed with Prof Chaddha. There was no need for that explanation.

'Sir, please have dinner with us,' Siddharth offered.

'Thank you, but I have a small job to attend to. I must leave now. Another day, perhaps.' Dr Chaddha left.

Siddharth had been told that Sylvia preferred food with little oil and spices. He had boiled some chicken for her. He would add some butter, ground pepper and salt and heat it in the microwave oven before serving it to her.

'I am not hungry. If you don't mind, I would like just a glass of milk,' Sylvia said.

'Yeah, sure!' Siddharth quickly brought her a glass of milk.

It was almost sunrise when she wished him goodnight and went to bed.

They met at the breakfast table next morning. She ate her eggs in a peculiar manner. She took a boiled egg with its shell unbroken and sawed it into two neat halves with a knife. Cupping the halves one by one she scooped out the egg with a spoon and put it in her mouth. Siddharth's amused gaze followed each half of the egg as the spoon and its contents disappeared into the small opening between Sylvia's soft, pink lips.

Sylvia had to go to different libraries in connection with her research project. Siddharth had to drop her at the library in the morning and pick her up again at five in the evening. After returning home, they watched TV and chatted lightly for some time. Later, they ate dinner and retired for the night. Sylvia talked about the small but beautiful town of Dresden where she was born. She told him that she did a part-time job selling tickets in an opera house at night and attended classes at the university during the day. She came across people from different walks of life and had several amusing experiences at the opera house. People came to the opera in formal outfits: men wore ties and hats and women gloves and wraps. It was interesting to see the same people who roamed about scantily dressed in briefs and shorts during summer so elaborately dressed for the opera.

It was probably the sixth day of Sylvia's stay in Siddharth's house. 'Would you like to go shopping?' Siddharth asked her. 'I am free today and could take you shopping in case you are interested.' Of course, she was delighted. They went to Palika Bazaar. Sylvia surveyed the items on display with a lot of interest. Their car was parked on the other side of the road. Siddhartha stepped off the arcade with Sylvia at his heels and began walking across the crowded road to the other side. Something prompted him to take a look back. He closed his eyes in fear at what he saw.

Sylvia stood in the middle of the road, thoroughly confused. Two big cars were rushing at her from either side, the drivers of both unnerved by her sudden appearance on the road. In less than a second, Siddharth ran back to where Sylvia stood, yelling 'Stop!' at the perilously advancing cars. With a superhuman effort, he swept Sylvia off the road, carrying her in his arms, and almost sailing through the jostling traffic, landed on the other side of the road. He looked at the rushing stream of traffic with unbelieving eyes for a couple of minutes, his heart racing.

'How could you be so careless?' he shouted at her, completely losing his temper out of sheer fright. 'Do you realize what could have happened?' Sylvia's face flushed red but she did not say anything.

'Why don't you answer me?' Siddharth went on obstinately. 'What would have happened if one of those cars had run over you?'

'Why are you getting so worked up?' she asked with a feeble smile. 'At the worst, I would have been martyred on Indian soil,' she added, trying to sound light-hearted.

'And for what act of bravery?' he demanded, still trying to control his temper.

'You could have held my hand and led me across the road instead of leaving me on my own,' she said softly and stretched out her right hand towards Siddharth. It was closed into a small fist. Without thinking, Siddharth gripped it in both hands. He did not let go of Sylvia's hand during the rest of the walk.

The incident seemed to have erased the slim line of unfamiliarity and brought them close to each other. That night, sitting at the dining table, Siddharth no longer felt discomfited. He had discovered a friend.

After dinner, they wished each other goodnight and went to sleep.

Originally, Sylvia was scheduled to go sight-seeing around Delhi on her own over the next two days and tickets had been purchased for her on a tourist bus. But now Siddharth had the tickets cancelled. He adjusted his classes, reshuffling his timetable, and took Sylvia sightseeing during the afternoons. They went to the Lal Quilla, to Rajghat, the Qutub Minar, and the Lotus Temple. The interest and enthusiasm that Sylvia revealed as she went round the monuments amazed Siddharth. He compelled her to eat at a restaurant, assuring her that it would be perfectly safe. Sylvia ate kulfi with great relish.

During the rest of her stay in Delhi, they spent most of the time in each other's company. They strolled along the winding paths of the Jawaharlal Nehru University and the IIT campuses, watched open-air theatre at Mandi House, and drank black coffee at the Indian Coffee House. Siddhartha told her about the history of Delhi, the growth of Hinduism, the coming of Islam, and the fall of the Moghul Empire. He also spoke about his home in Bhubaneswar, the sea beach at Puri, and the sun temple at Konark. Sylvia spoke with feeling about the rift between East and West Germany, which her elders had told her about. She spoke of the ideological and psychological differences between the two Germanys and the eagerness of both to get reunited. She said she had heard people say that the lovely city of Dresden was the pride of East Germany, but most of the splendid medieval forts, towering churches, and opera houses had been destroyed during the Second World War. Now, of course, Sylvia said, the government was making serious efforts to rebuild these historical structures and restore to the city its historical importance. Sylvia talked about her father, who, she said, was deeply learned and wise. He was a great admirer of oriental culture and she had inherited his fascination with the East. Germans have great love for their own language and are not much interested in learning English, she said. She also told him when and how she had learnt English.

'Sidar, I would like to see the Taj Mahal,' she said one day. 'Father had asked me not to miss it.' There was a compelling appeal in her voice.

Sylvia could never pronounce Siddharth's name right. It was 'Sidarat' in the beginning, but later she abbreviated it to a simpler 'Sidar', which was easier for her to pronounce.

'He was right,' Siddharth agreed. 'Let's plan the visit for tomorrow.'

The thought that in only three days, Sylvia would leave India nagged him intermittently, filling him with sadness.

They started the four-hour drive to Agra at six the next morning, carrying with them an airbag stuffed with food: bread and jam, boiled eggs, fruits, and bottled water.

They stopped first at the Agra Fort.

Sylvia marvelled at the sight of the fort. 'What a colossal structure!' she exclaimed in wonder. There were innumerable chambers and halls, each different from the other in its décor. Siddharth took her to the bank of the Yamuna. She stood by the dome on its bank and looked at its enormous expanse. The water glittered in the sunlight. What grandeur! The Yamuna that Siddharth had shown her at Delhi looked like a mere trickle compared to this magnificent stream. Sylvia was spellbound by all that she saw.

Thin clouds of dust drifted towards them from the sandy banks of the Yamuna. Siddharth pointed at the Taj Mahal silhouetted in the haze.

'Let's go there first,' Sylvia urged.

'No, we shall eat first,' said Siddharth.

Sylvia stared in disbelief at the majestic monument.

'What unimaginable beauty! Truly a poem in marble!' she soliloquized dreamily.

Siddharth watched her fondly, enjoying her bewilderment.

'The Moghul emperor Shah Jahan got this mausoleum built in memory of his beloved queen Mumtaz Mahal, who had died prematurely, as a symbol of their love.' Siddharth explained.

'Such a massive memorial dedicated to his wife!' Sylvia looked at Siddharth with incredulous eyes. 'How he must have loved her!' Sylvia's eyes brimmed over with emotion.

The sunlight fell directly on Sylvia, framing her face in a soft glow. She was like a freshly bloomed flower. Siddharth took his eyes away with an effort.

On the way back to Delhi, both were unusually quiet. Siddharth drove rather absentmindedly. A sense of closeness that would have been difficult to describe had arisen between them. It was like the subtle fragrance of an expensive perfume that hung in the air but never drew attention to itself. No words were needed to express the feeling.

Later, in the silence of the winter night, Siddharth stood at the window in the dining room, looking through the curtains at a large pond in the distance. He could not see the water. A thick patch of fog that got thinner at the top hung over the surface. A gust of icy wind rushed into the room through the window, sending a chill through Siddharth. A feeling of loneliness made him shiver. His throat felt dry. He could not recollect when they had reached home or what they had had for dinner. Sylvia filled his mind, leaving no room for any other thought. He felt she had been with him for a long, long time. Neither past nor future existed for him—only the enigmatic moments of their togetherness, creating a permanent 'now', mattered. Siddharth wanted it to last forever, realizing at the same time that soon it would be time to say goodbye. He stood at the window, face to face with the bitter-sweet moment of truth, watching helplessly the wavering world he had built up before she came into his life. He pressed his face against the window pane as if battling with himself in the dark for the last time before admitting defeat.

'Sidar,' Sylvia spoke softly out of the darkness, touching his shoulder gently. Siddharth winced. 'Don't touch me.' His voice was a feeble scream.

She drew her hand away instantly, startled at the reaction. Siddharth turned and looked directly at her. Even in the darkness, he could see her delicate eyelids heavy with hurt.

'Please don't touch me!' Siddharth begged. He was not sure if he really wanted to say that.

Before Sylvia even raised her head to look at him, Siddharth, with a force that was greater than all other compulsive urges he had ever experienced, pulled her towards him. Without saying a word, Sylvia hid her face in his chest.

They remained indoors all through the next day. Sylvia prepared chicken stew and Siddharth got a bottle of champagne to go with it. He lit a candle on the dining table and put a cassette in the music system. The mellifluous tune of Chaurasia's flute floated in like ripples of serenity. They sat in silence, listening to the soothing music. The clock on the wall ticked. Siddharth's eyes kept returning to the clock, aware that moment after moment of the most wonderful period of his life was flitting away. The melancholic note of the flute filled him with a terrible sense of loss. Siddharth made a conscious effort to put it out of his mind.

'Sidar, you are just wonderful!' Sylvia said fondly. Leaving her chair, she came to stand behind him. She wound her delicate arms around his neck and, leaning forward, rested her chin on his head. The words of fond admiration combined with her adoring gesture transported Siddharth to a level of experience that he never believed existed.

The day of parting dawned.

Siddharth found her busy packing when he entered her room in the afternoon. The floor and the bed were littered with several items that Siddharth had gifted her and things she had picked up during her visits to places. She picked them up one by one and put them in her suitcase. She paused at her work as she saw Siddharth coming near her. 'Will you come to Dresden some time?' she asked, looking up at him.

He nodded weakly.

'We shall stroll along the bank of the river Elbe. It is a lovely river of crystal-clear water, slim enough to be confused with a creek. We shall walk together on the sandy patch along the waterline.' She stopped to look again at Siddharth.

It was as if he was about to lose a precious object that had been in his possession for some time and which he had come to believe was his very own. He had absolutely no idea where and how to retrieve it.

'What do you say? Will you come there?' Sylvia repeated. Siddharth did not say a word. Perhaps he could not trust his voice.

It was time to leave for the airport. Dr Chaddha arrived and asked them to hurry.

Siddharth's unblinking eyes followed Sylvia as she walked towards the security check area. The most promising moments of his life, cast in human form in a pair of jeans and a blue T-shirt, were moving out of reach. Just before entering the gate at the security check, Sylvia turned round and waved. Even from that distance, Siddharth guessed that a few tears were trickling down her eyes. He wanted to scream at the top of his voice, 'Come back, Sylvia! Don't leave me alone,' but no words came. Sylvia had disappeared out of sight.

The delicate smell of her perfume still lingered. Siddharth inhaled deeply and closed his eyes. He felt the presence of someone very dear all around him. 'Sidar, you are just wonderful,' a voice seemed to whisper in his ear.

The strident ring of the phone brought him back to earth. He lifted the receiver unmindfully.

'Hello.'

'Weren't you home?' Minati sounded worried. 'I have been calling you for quite some time now.'

'Oh yes, I had gone to the airport to see Sylvia off.'

'Who?'

'Didn't I tell you about her? The German girl that Dr Chaddha insisted I accommodate in our house.'

There was a small, thoughtful pause. 'Yes, I remember. But she should not have stayed there in my absence. It does not look right. Why couldn't Dr Chaddha take her to his home?' There was a note of accusation in her voice.

'I understand,' Siddharth said, making an effort to sound normal. 'But Dr Chaddha almost compelled me. You know how it is!' He tried to explain. Minati said nothing. Siddharth changed the subject. 'How is Pupun? And how are you? You must take care of your own health.' The undertone of guilt was unmistakable in his voice.

'I can't take it that easily,' Minati said ignoring Siddharth's explanation. 'I will definitely speak to Dr Chaddha about this.' There was the sound of a faint click at the other end.

The Nowhere Nest

'Ma, where is my silver *kajal pati*?'

'Shhh!' Her mother pressed a warning finger to her lips as she came out of the kitchen, wiping her right hand on the end of her saree. 'Your younger sister-in-law took it; she said she liked its design.' She came up close and spoke in a conspiratorial whisper, as if revealing a secret.

'And the granite image of the goddess that was on my table?'

'Oh, that! I gave that away to the elder one—you know how keen she is on collecting things like that; she has quite an assortment of images of deities.' She paused and looked at her daughter for a moment. Her eyes softened. 'You should have taken your things away much earlier, Sushree,' she said consolingly. 'Termites got into most of your books and the notebooks in which you jotted down your songs. I saved what I could and packed them away in a box. Have a look at the things and take them with you.'

Sushree's restless eyes swept round the room. Where was her sitar? She didn't see it anywhere. Could it be lying under one of the beds? When had she seen it last? Must be about ten years ago. Her mother had wrapped it up in an old sari and put it away in a corner of the room that had been hers before her marriage, when she was doing her BA. It wasn't there now. Ma must have put it away somewhere.

'Ma, my sitar used to be in this room. Have you moved it elsewhere?' she asked. There was a tinge of apprehension in her voice.

'Shree, surely you don't need it now? It was so old it was falling apart! The boys next door started a music school and went from door to door collecting money and old instruments. Your father suggested we donate the sitar to the school.' Her voice sounded guilty. 'But that was almost five or six years ago.'

True. Sushree hadn't even looked at the sitar for the last five or six years, although she had been coming back at least once every year, if only for a couple of days. It had been ages since she had seen the sitar, wrapped in a dirty old sari, leaning against the wall in a corner, half hidden among the cobwebs. Her father had passed away three years ago. The old, abandoned sitar had been forgotten amid the anxiety and grief of his illness and death.

Still, Ma could have asked her once! They spoke to each other almost every day over the phone, on all kinds of topics, important as well as trivial. Her mother had become lonely with the years. Her own life was lonely too but they didn't talk to each other directly about their loneliness, trying to keep it at bay, and chatted away on other topics instead: Ajay has so much work in the office these days that he returns home late; our daughter has been insisting that we go to Mumbai for a holiday but he just can't get away. Ma would talk about her two daughters-in-law: they were seldom to be found at home. One of her sons had high blood pressure and the other a sprained ankle. She talked about her grandchildren, about the neighbours. Someone was unwell and someone else had to cut a pilgrimage short on account of sudden illness.

Somebody's granddaughter had gone to America for higher studies and surprised everyone by calling up to announce she was getting married.

Loneliness hovered over the lives of both, threatening at times to come down and touch them. Sushree tried to shrug it off. Ajay was becoming distant: he rarely spoke to her when he came home—as though she was just a piece of the wall! He would rush off to the club after a quick shower, returning late, often drunk. Then he had a hurried bite and went to sleep. Sometimes he would ask her if she wanted to come with him but she was too proud to say yes. So it was when he woke up in the morning too: he picked up his cup of tea and buried himself in a corner with his newspapers.

None of this did she share with her mother.

The two daughters-in-law were absorbed in their own world—just they, their husbands, and their children. To them, Ma was an outsider—as if meals and old-age medicines were all the care she needed!

But she never mentioned any of this to Sushree.

But why had Ma said nothing about the silver kajal-pati, the granite image, or the sitar? Maybe she hadn't thought it necessary; she had assumed that Sushree would have no further use for these things. She didn't know how strongly attached Sushree was to her childhood possessions.

She had almost forgotten about the things, never thought of them consciously. But she had never dreamt that that they would simply disappear from her home.

Her home!

Yes, this had been her home, from the day she was born to the day she sat for the BA examination. Then came her marriage. A married daughter was supposed to visit her parents' home, alone or with her husband, for no more than two or three days at a time. The exception was made only when her children were to be born; then, she could stay for two or three months.

The three of them—her elder brother, whom she called Bhaina, she, and Mohan, the youngest—had slept in the same room when they were very small, on two beds that had been joined together. At study time, they were lined up on a straw mat spread on the floor, while the tutor, common to all three, squatted on an *asana*. Bhaina was two years older and Mohan a year and a half younger. Ma would fold their clothes neatly and hang them on the same wooden *alana*, kept in the veranda.

Ma was constantly worried because the house was too small. Sushree's parents slept in one room and her grandparents in another. There was a tiny outer room, which her father used for his medical practice; in the evenings, he sat in a room that was part of a medicine shop in the bazaar. She had been in the eighth class then. That year, her grandfather died. Her father took a one-roomed cottage in the bazaar on rent and started his own clinic. The outer room was turned into a study for Bhaina and Mohan. *Jeji ma* moved into the room with Sushree and her room was given to the two brothers.

'Why should *Nani* have that large room all to herself?' Mohan had complained.

'How long is she going to remain there? She's a girl, after all—she'll get married and go away. Won't it become *your* room then?' her mother said, running her fingers affectionately through Mohan's hair.

'Let her be there,' Bhaina said. 'She's not going to be there alone—Jeji Ma will share it with her. And *Jeje Bapa*'s ghost as well.' He winked at Mohan mischievously.

Sushree said nothing; she didn't know what to say. Things were different with Jeji Ma around. When she went to sleep, there was an unending flood of stories and reminiscences from the past. Life went on slowly, lazily, for almost six years—until she was married.

There were friends from her days in school and college. The best of her school friends was Damini. She did not have much interest in studies but she was very affectionate. Every day, she brought something tasty from her home for Sushree to eat. She often stayed over for the night in Sushree's room, and then Jeji Ma went and slept in her grandsons' bed. 'The two of you are going to gossip all night,' she told the girls. 'I won't get any sleep in that room.'

What was it they had talked about? Sushree could not remember. They had probably been weaving dreams in the darkness as they lay on the bed....

They were in the eleventh class. Winter was ending and the exams were imminent. They had been warned that they must study seriously and so Damini and she were together for joint study. Sushree still had vivid memories of those days. On Sunday, Damini came home with some sour oranges, climbed onto the bed, and promptly sat down next to the window. She looked unusually grave. Before she could say anything, Sushree got busy arranging salt, garlic, and green chillies in a stainless steel bowl. They sat facing each other with the sour oranges in the middle. After an awkward silence, Damini confided that she was in love with someone.

He was fourteen years older, married with three children, and ran a stationery shop in the bazaar. They had vowed to get married—or else they would swallow some yellow oleander seeds and end their lives.

Sushree's eyes grew wide with surprise and her mouth remained open, the slice of sour orange forgotten. She had never expected to hear this strange confession. She hadn't had any thoughts of love yet; besides, her two brothers kept close watch on her. She wasn't allowed to speak to any boy.

All she could say, after a fairly long pause, was, 'What about his wife and children?'

'Nothing will change for them,' Damini answered. 'I will bring up the children as my own, and I have promised him I will never have children of my own.' Her eyes were sparkling.

Sushree could only stare at her in surprise. Damini had suddenly acquired a new stature in her eyes; what she was telling her related to a very different world, far removed from the narrow confines of their friendship. She had been unable to sleep for a long time after Damini left. Damini had undergone a transforming experience and entered a new world but she—she had stood still. She had a strange feeling of envy. What self-confidence her friend had!

The results were announced. Sushree had obtained a first division but Damini had got a bare pass. Damini was two years older. She didn't continue her studies. They seldom met now. Sushree found new friends in college and nearly forgot about Damini. On the day her Intermediate results were to be announced, Damini's brother came to their home carrying an invitation card. Damini was getting married. Her husband-to-be was a clerk in some government office in Cuttack. On the day of the wedding, Sushree went up to Damini as she sat dressed in bridal clothes, and whispered into her ear, 'And what about the shopkeeper?' Damini had smiled feebly. There wasn't much news of her, but shortly after Sushree's last visit to her mother's home in Sambalpur, she heard that Damini was no more. Cancer had claimed her.

Sushree's parents had started looking for a match for her even before she appeared for the BA examination. She would hear of various prospective bridegrooms; finally, her parents decided on Ajay. He was six years older than her, came from a respectable family, and had a good job. A few months later, they were married.

After her father's death, Sushree's mother had moved to her room and mother and daughter shared the room when Sushree came home on one of her periodical visits. She came home this time because Ma wanted her to.

In the afternoon, when both of them were relaxing on the bed, her mother said to her, 'Shree, I had told you over the phone that Saroj (her elder son) and Mohan are planning to get this house renovated. That's what their wives want as well. Two new rooms will be added and this older portion of the house will be demolished. The work will start very soon—maybe in the next four or five days. That was why I asked you to come home urgently, in case any of your personal belongings are still lying in this house. You will not see it in its present shape again. They are going to make this a three-storeyed house. The ground floor will be rented out; Saroj will occupy the first floor and Mohan the top floor. I have packed all your things into two crates. You can rest now and take a look at them in the evening.' Her mother took a deep breath.

'And you? Where will you live?' Sushree asked her mother anxiously.

'Oh, there won't be any problem for me. I'll spend a few days with Saroj and then a few days with Mohan. While the construction is going on, a part of the veranda can be partitioned off with wire mesh and my bed put there.' Her voice was calm. She seemed resigned to all that was happening and was able to tell her daughter about it with equal calmness.

So the two brothers are going to live separately! But no one had thought of informing her. Bhaina had become a lecturer in a private college in Sambalpur and Mohan was in the real estate business. So far, they had lived together. How easily they had decided Ma's future! Surely, they could never have spared a thought for her. Once this house was demolished, she would be without a parental home. True, she had not owned the place, but she had enjoyed the privileges of a daughter. But if such was her mother's condition in the new scheme of things, what hope was there that some arrangement would be made for her?

What things did you want me to look at, Ma?

What have you packed for me in bundles?

What shall I carry away? Memories of childhood quarrels with my brothers, eating pakhala with schoolmates on the veranda? Listening to the cuckoo's song through the window? Closing my eyes and inhaling the fragrance of baula blossoms after the rain? Sobbing to myself at the foot of the mango tree in the yard when my marriage was fixed? The stories I told my children of my own childhood?

She had lived many more years outside that home than she had spent in it. What claims did she have now on that silver kajal-pati, the granite goddess, or the sitar?

Where was her trunk? The one made of zinc sheets?

'Ma, where is my zinc trunk?' she asked suddenly, sitting up in bed. 'Is it under the bed?'

'No,' her mother replied, without opening her eyes. 'It's in the garage, along with all the other old trunks and boxes. The elder daughter-in-law wanted them dumped there, since there was no fear of termites damaging them.'

'I'll bring it back here,' Sushree said, getting up.

'Wait,' her mother said. 'The servant is taking a nap. I shall ask him to get it from the garage when we are having our afternoon tea.'

Sushree lay back on the bed again, feeling relaxed. But sleep would not come.

When the servant carried the trunk into the room and put it down on the floor that evening, she sat up at once. She had not joined the others for tea but had carried her cup of tea into the room. As soon as the servant left, she got up and bolted the room from inside. She had forgotten all about that trunk! Quickly, she sat down on the floor next to it.

The trunk had two locks, one at each end. One of the clasps was missing; the other had been secured with a lock she had never seen before. 'That's not my lock!' Sushree said to herself, examining it closely. She took a key out of her handbag and tried to unlock it. No! It wouldn't open. So both locks had been tampered with! The trunk had been broken open. It must be the doing of her sisters-in-law. They must have opened the box and gone through its contents with great curiosity. Her ears reddened with anger.

'Ma!' she called out. 'The lock on this trunk isn't the one I had put on it. Where is its key?'

Her elder sister-in-law entered the room. 'We had to open the trunk to check what was inside, just in case it had got spoilt,' she said. 'I've kept the key carefully. Here it is, Shree.' She turned and walked out of the room quickly, as if some urgent work awaited her. Was there a mocking smile on her lips? How dare they open my trunk without asking me? Sushree was getting restless.

She bolted the door once again and sat down to open the trunk. The lock opened easily. Slowly, she lifted the lid. It was like a casket of fond memories opening before her eyes. She examined the things inside with delicate hands— trifles that had been so precious to her once. Three or four certificates, which she had received for sports or dramatics; a landscape she had painted while at school; small embroidered handkerchiefs; a thriller titled *Bandit Queen Meera*, with peacock feathers between the pages for bookmarks; a doll that she had played with as a child; a notebook that contained some half-written poems; some letters that Ajay had written to her shortly after their marriage....

But there was something else that she was looking for desperately. It was the sudden thought that her sisters-in-law might have opened her trunk in her absence and discovered it that had upset and enraged her. Her hands groped feverishly under the odds and ends in the trunk until she found it—a small leather bag, lying at the bottom. With one quick movement, she pulled the zip open and looked inside. She had believed that this trunk in her mother's home would be the safest place to hide Sarat's letters!

Sushree sat on the floor, leaning against the bed, holding the bag. She wiped the beads of sweat from her face with her saree and let out a sigh. She took out one of the letters and opened it....

She had been a teacher in a school at Rourkela, having taken up teaching rather late in life. Her son was born a year after her marriage and the daughter came two years later. Her husband had been transferred three times within those few years. It was only after her daughter's birth that she thought of joining the BEd classes and becoming a teacher. Her husband made all the arrangements. She was first posted to the government middle English school at Cuttack. Ajay was transferred to Rourkela after three years. Sushree applied for a transfer to Rourkela and went on leave so she could accompany Ajay to Rourkela. Her posting orders came after three months and she joined the middle English school at Rourkela. Her son was in high school by that time. Sushree got her daughter admitted to the same school where she was teaching. Sarat was teaching mathematics there.

They were assigned the duty of conducting a drawing and singing competition for the children. She had barely met Sarat before that. He had done his MA in Mathematics from Utkal University and was a bachelor—that was all she knew about him. But something happened that day that brought them closer. School was over. Sushree and her daughter were about to start for home. Suddenly, dark clouds filled the sky and it started raining heavily. How would she get home? Ajay's jeep wouldn't be available since he was away on tour. Sarat suggested she take a rickshaw. Sushree and her daughter went home in the pouring rain with Sarat escorting them on his bicycle. Sushree asked him inside but he said he had to go. That day, he had revealed to her that he was not happy about being a teacher.

The memory was still fresh. Sarat and she grew closer every day; then, without her knowing it, fondness turned into love. Sarat did not have a phone at home and used to call from public booths. Sushree sat waiting by her phone for his calls for hours, fearful that Ajay might pick up the phone. Despite her warnings, Sarat wrote long love letters—letters that told of the urgency of passion, the agony of separation, and the hope of fulfilment. Sushree used to read his letters over and over.

After a lot of persuasion, she went to meet Sarat in his single-roomed apartment. She could still recall the tingle of that experience: the fear of being discovered while she tapped softly on the door, entering quickly as soon as the door opened, and hiding her face in Sarat's chest as he held her tightly in his arms. All the while, she felt herself fighting some invisible enemy. She recollected the hurt anger in Sarat's voice when she told him these secret meetings had to stop. 'Very well,' he said. 'Just as you like!' The experience had lasted for eight and a half months.

The principal called Sarat to his office one day when no one else was present and told him about the rumours he was picking up. The school was getting a bad name, he warned Sarat. A few days later, Ajay announced that he had been transferred back to Cuttack. He would have to join the very next day. Sushree went on long leave again. Ajay returned a couple of days later, and within a few days, all of them shifted to Cuttack. Sushree did not understand why Ajay was transferred back to Cuttack so abruptly. Had he volunteered for it? The rumour might have reached his ears too. But Ajay never mentioned anything. Sushree had wept until late in the night after Ajay left for Cuttack. She spent the entire afternoon next day at Sarat's house.

Despite Sarat's repeated requests, Sushree had never replied to his letters. After three letters, he had stopped writing. She came to know later that after two years of her return to Cuttack, Sarat had got married. He had also got a job in a bank.

Had all this really happened to her? It seemed so unreal.

It had lasted only eight months. But how crowded those months had been! She had somehow believed that the memories could be stored away safely in that old trunk, coated with zinc, in her parental home. She had put the letters in the leather bag, hidden the bag in the trunk, and locked it.

She called Ajay from her cell phone: 'You wanted to know if I needed the car? I would like to leave this place tomorrow morning. Can you send the car by ten thirty?'

Sushree's younger sister-in-law looked through the half-open door as the driver was keeping the trunk in the boot of the car. 'What do you need that old trunk for, Nani?' she asked with feigned ignorance. 'Let me take it back to the garage.'

'It will come in handy for storing some of the junk I have at home,' Sushree answered without looking at her and got into the car. She asked the driver to drive her to the market but did not get off there. Then she asked him to make a detour on the highway and finally stopped at the bridge over the Koel River. Getting out of the car, Sushree walked up to the railings and looked down. The wide stream flowed serenely below her. She asked the driver to take the trunk out of the luggage boot. He looked at her questioningly. Before he could say a thing, Sushree carried the trunk to the edge of the bridge. She placed it on the railing for support, took a deep breath, and gave the trunk a light push. Down it went, falling into the water with a loud splash.

A part of her life that should have been solely hers had been drowned.

Everything about her house in Bhubaneswar seemed unfamiliar to Sushree as she stepped into it. After a whole chapter of one's life has been wiped clean, people and places suddenly appear unreal, strange, don't they?

Could she call even this house her own? She felt she was just a lifeless part of the house, like its walls, its ceiling, doors and windows. Scenes from days long past flashed before her eyes as she entered the house. She was standing by a wall, leaning on it and wiping her hands with her saree. There was Ajay eating breakfast, his eyes hovering on the open pages of the newspaper. Hadn't she always been used as a supporting wall by her husband and children? But she could never be the whole house! Her thoughts floated back to her wedding night. 'I always sleep on the right side of the bed,' Ajay had announced, coming out of the bathroom as Sushree sat arranging her clothes in the late hours of the night.

It sounded a little out of place to Sushree. She remembered she used to sleep on a particular side of the bed when Jeji Ma and she had shared the room. But she quickly walked round the bed to the other side as soon as Ajay had indicated his preference. Ajay always sat at in the same chair at the dining table, facing a particular direction and had his favourite sofa in the drawing room, always sat at on the left side in the car's rear seat. He asked Sushree to move if, by any chance, she sat in his place. He had never compromised.

What difference do these little things make? Let the children and their father stick to their habits if they want to, what harm can there be? Does it really matter which side of the bed you sleep on? Sushree said to herself.

She wondered why those memories were coming back to her now. She had reconciled herself to everything and catered to every need of her children and husband. They needed her more to fill a gap than for anything else.

In the beginning, she had enjoyed the transfers, the experience of moving from one place to another. Later, it became difficult. It was painful to leave a place just when one had developed an attachment. But she never looked back, never tried to retrieve the memories she was leaving behind when the household articles were being loaded onto the truck. She had taken these things for granted.

'I must tell you something,' Ajay's excited voice brought Sushree back to the present. 'I couldn't mention it this morning as I was in a hurry to leave for the office.' He sat down on the sofa to explain.

'I am due to retire in two years. We'll move to Puri after my retirement. I have booked a three-bedroom apartment there. The property developer has agreed to buy this house and give us four flats in Puri in exchange. Life is easier in an apartment. There will be no office peons once I retire and you know how difficult it is to find a domestic help these days. You will enjoy Puri. What could be more relaxing than spending the rest of our life in Lord Jagannath's shadow?' He paused for a while and asked the peon for a glass of water. 'Of the four apartments, we shall keep two for the children and one for us and sell the fourth.' He went on, as if anticipating her thoughts, 'No, not now. Only after my retirement.'

Sushree didn't want to hear any more. Ajay had planned everything and never even asked her! What about her? Had he asked her what she wanted? She had six more years of service. Should she go on long leave yet again or apply for voluntary retirement? But why worry? As always, he would have the perfect solution for her!

She wanted to shout, 'Who are you to decide for me?' but instead she said, 'Do whatever you think right,' smiling feebly and going into the kitchen to make tea.

They had been living in their own house for the last three years. They would live there for two more years, according to Ajay's calculations. After two years, they would move into their own apartment at Puri. Ajay had built the house but Sushree had made it a home. She had talked to the concrete, to the bricks and cement and steel. Ajay had only given the orders; it was she who had accepted each inanimate part of the house as a living member. The plants in the garden were beginning to bloom. Fruits had appeared on the papaya trees; the lychee and sapodilla plum plants would follow suit very soon. She had tended the plants like her own children. How could she part with them? But could Ajay understand?

'Mani is seriously ill. She has been asking me for a long time to come to Delhi and see her. I am applying for leave from school. Will you please make a reservation for tomorrow on the Rajdhani Express?' Sushree said to Ajay next morning as they were having tea. Mani was Sushree's cousin, who lived in Delhi. She had not been well for some time and had been urging Sushree to visit her.

'Is that right?' Ajay said. 'You never told me! Do you have to go in such haste?' He lifted his eyes from the newspaper and looked questioningly at her.

'Yes,' she said. 'Get the reservation, please.' Sushree looked into Ajay's eyes as she spoke.

'Okay, remind me at the office.' His eyes returned to the newspaper. 'How long are you going to be in Delhi?' he asked without looking at her.

'Just a few days,' Sushree replied lightly. She knew Ajay would not ask another question.

Next day, Sushree boarded the Rajdhani Express. Ajay came to the railway station to see her off. Sushree could sense that he was a little worried about something. 'Did you ring them up and give them the number of your coach and berth? Are you sure someone will pick you up at the station?' he asked, as the train was about to leave. 'Yes,' Sushree said, 'but you can ring up and remind them.' Ajay nodded. The train left the station.

☙

'Where are you? I have been trying for hours to reach you on your phone but it was switched off! Ajay is almost hysterical. My husband looked for you at the station but the conductor said you weren't on the train and must have got off at some midway station. Where did you get off?' Mani blabbered over the phone breathlessly without waiting for a reply.

'You know, Mani, I drifted off to sleep and had a beautiful dream! When I woke up, I found myself at this lovely place, surrounded by high mountains. It's so peaceful! I just dipped my feet in the icy waters of the Ganga. Shall I tell you about my dream? I dreamt I had been transformed into a bird—something like a kingfisher or a golden oriole. I was soaring into the blue sky, flying high up in the air. I kept flying on and on and never wanted to come down. Everything, the trees, the mountains and houses, remained far below me—'

'Shree nani, are you all right? Where are you? Please tell me! We've been worried sick! My husband and I will reach you as soon as you tell us where you are. Your children have not been told of this until now. Nani, are you there? Can you hear me?'

'It was such a lovely dream, Mani! I wish I could have slept a little longer,' Sushree said as she disconnected the phone.

Her Best Friend Jaya

'Listen, could you wake up a little early in the morning tomorrow?' Itishree asked her husband as they lay in bed.

'Why?' Bikash asked irritably.

'Jaya is arriving by the Tapaswini Express. We have to receive her at the railway station,' Itishree explained, trying not to sound too eager.

'Take the driver with you. I can't get up so early,' Bikash muttered sleepily and turned over on his side.

'The driver had already left when Jaya called. How could I have told him?'

'Who is this Jaya anyway?' Bikash asked and, without waiting for an answer, continued. 'I don't understand why so many people from different places have to come to see you. She must be coming to get some problem of hers solved through my intervention. As though the government employs me only to do such things!' he grumbled.

'You mustn't speak like that,' Itishree retorted. 'Shouldn't we help our own people when they are in trouble? Jaya was my best friend in college. What is there to be so upset about if she asks for a little help? Thousands of outsiders get their work done through your influence, but you refuse to help when I ask you to do something for me!' Her voice was thick with emotion.

'Do you know,' she went on, 'we were roommates in the hostel. There were two beds but we shared one. We used to eat from the same plate! We were always together. Everyone in the hostel called us "the mynah pair". She was married six months earlier than I and that was why she couldn't attend my wedding. She couldn't come even for the *ekoisia* of our son Jeetu. Her one-year-old daughter was down with diarrhoea at that time. We haven't met for the last five years, but I am as much to blame as she is. I've just been too busy to keep up the contact.'

Bikash, however, was snoring by this time and missed the elaborate narration.

It was only when he woke up the next morning that the gravity of what Itishree had said last night was impressed upon him. She had driven herself to the station to receive her friend without waking him up. He experienced a mild sting of self-reproach. He shouldn't have let her go on her own in that chaotic traffic.

She returned as Bikash was leaving for the office. 'I didn't use your office car,' she said in a tone that was a complaint as well as accusation, and walked into the dining hall.

'You should have woken me up,' Bikash said, trying to sound conciliatory. 'I was worried when you were so late in coming back.'

'Never mind,' Itishree said. 'I just stopped at Nimapara Sweets on the way back to pick up some *chhenapoda*. Jaya loves it.' She turned and pulled the woman who stood half hidden behind her to the front. 'Meet Jaya Panda,' she said, 'the other mynah in the pair. You *have* seen her photograph but I am sure you don't remember.'

The woman whom his wife introduced joined her palms together in a namaskar, a sweet smile hovering on her lips. Bikash observed that she was slim and a little taller than Itishree. Less fair than Itishree, Jaya had a dusky complexion.

'She has been singing your praises all the way home,' Jaya said. 'There's no one in the world quite like you, according to her.' She looked directly into Bikash's eyes and her lips curved in a small smile.

'Oh, come on,' said Itishree. 'You can't get away with that smooth talk. I haven't forgiven you yet for not coming to my wedding. You must have been enjoying a prolonged honeymoon! And as for Bikash, just wait until I reveal his true profile to you!' Itishree's face glowed with affection for her husband as she made the fond complaint.

'I guess my reputation isn't going to recover from this assault! Well, can't be helped, I suppose. That's the way my stars are!' Bikash said with a smile, looking at his wife. He flicked a hurried glance at the wall clock and walked to the front door. 'I will send the car in case you need it,' he said as he walked out through the door.

'Yes, do that. I have taken the day off. We will go shopping.' Itishree looked at Jaya and smiled.

The two friends went through the family album containing photographs taken on various occasions, beginning with Itishree's wedding and ending with her son's recent birthday. They gossiped endlessly all through the day, ate, and reminisced nostalgically about their college days.

'Do you know?' Jaya said. 'Tania and her husband are divorced.'

'Yes, I heard. They say her husband had been living with another woman and married her soon after their divorce.'

'Do you remember that dark-complexioned girl with long, thick hair—the one who had the room facing ours? She committed suicide.'

'And that slim, handsome boy in the English department, the one with the dreamy eyes, remember him? How he and Sagarika talked for hours under the *gulmohar* tree in front of the girls' hostel! But she didn't marry him finally. Strange, isn't it?'

'Then, there was that boy from the Department of Statistics who followed us to our hostel every day as we returned after classes. I used to tease you, saying he was after you! We had named him Majnu, the lover, do you remember? I met him in the bus once sometime back. He had changed, looked smart. He smiled when he saw me. He is a lecturer now in some college near Sambalpur, he said, and asked how I was.'

They talked and talked, one topic leading to another, trying to revive the past. The chain of subjects kept growing unstoppably. It seemed fifty years had passed since their last meeting, not just five.

Jaya rose to her feet, yawned, and stretched her arms. 'Doesn't Bikash Babu come home for lunch?' she asked.

'No need to be so formal!' Itishree admonished her friend. '"Bikash" will do. No, not regularly. I am generally busy with college work and cannot give him company. I ask him to have lunch at home only when I've cooked something special. He won't come today, I am sure, because you are here. He's very shy by nature.'

'Too bad he has to eat out on account of me! Why don't you ask him to come over for lunch?' Jaya suggested. She sounded concerned.

'Not today. Some other day perhaps. Let us spend the day gossiping to our heart's content. And remember, I shall not let you leave before a week.'

'No, darling, I have left my little daughter with her father. I can't afford to stay more than four or five days. But please get my work done soon—the poor boy is really in trouble....'

'My God! It's almost evening,' Itishree exclaimed, glancing at the clock. 'We were so busy talking that we lost track of time. Let me see what we have by way of snacks. Shall I get some dosa from the South Indian restaurant nearby? It is famous for its dosa. My son would love to have dosa when he comes back after playing. I shall get some.'

'Won't it be a bother?'

'Not at all. The cook will get it for us.' Itishree got up and made her way to the kitchen. The horn of a car was heard outside as Itishree was coming out of the kitchen. Bikash took off his shoes and entered the room, pushing the curtain aside. Jaya undid her knotted hair and let her long, sleek tresses slither down her back. She adjusted the end of her sari that passed over her shoulder and stood up.

'How did you spend the day?' Bikash asked, looking at his wife although the question was meant for Jaya. Jaya laughed and answered, 'What do you expect? All Iti could talk about was you!'

'Oh, really!' Bikash exclaimed, his gaze fixed on Jaya. In reply, she laughed again, her eyes sparkling with mischief.

'I think the dosa has arrived. Let me see. The two of you can carry on with your chat.' Itishree walked back to the kitchen. Jaya stepped into her slippers and made her way towards the settee, dragging her feet across the fluffy drawing-room carpet. As she was about to sit down, she lurched forward a little. The end of her sari slipped from her shoulder onto the carpeted floor. She uttered a soft 'ahh', picked it up, and passed it carelessly over her left shoulder.

'Did you stumble?' Bikash asked anxiously.

'No, no, it was nothing.' Jaya looked at Bikash with a coy smile in her eyes.

'You must be tired after the day's work,' Jaya said to Bikash. 'I am sure it must be quite strenuous? That's why I decided not to take up a job.' They sat facing each other. 'How do you manage to work so hard? What do you do to handle the stress?' she asked as she raised her arms languidly to gather up her hair in and wind it into a knot at the nape of her neck. Bikash's eyes fell involuntarily on her upraised arms, the circular patch of sweat on the underarm of her blouse, and the outlines of the bulge on its right where the sari had slipped away. He quickly looked away and wiped his face with both his palms. 'It cannot be helped,' he said a little hoarsely. 'We have to do our duty after all.' Another soft smile danced on Jaya's lips. Bikash could smell the fragrance of her perfume.

He ate his dinner silently without taking his eyes off the plate and retreated into the safety of his bedroom, lay down on the bed, and began to leaf through the pages of a magazine.

Itishree came in sometime later.

'Jaya's father died of a heart attack last year, two years before his retirement,' she informed him. 'He was an assistant engineer, working in a project somewhere near Sambalpur. Jaya is the eldest child in the family. Her younger brother has graduated but is without a job. The youngest sister is in the second year of college. Jaya has to shoulder the responsibility of the entire family.'

Bikash did not say anything. His eyes kept hovering on the pages of the magazine.

'Why don't you say anything?' Itishree insisted.

'What is there to say?' Bikash said, glancing at his wife for a brief moment and turned his eyes to the page he was reading.

'I think we should do something to help the family. Her brother has applied for a job on compassionate grounds in the same office where his father was employed. He should have got it under the rehabilitation scheme. It is your department that deals with such matters. Jaya is confident that her brother could be recruited easily if you take a little initiative.'

'I can't recollect any such file being sent to me for approval.'

'I don't blame you for not remembering the case,' Itishree remonstrated. 'But when I ask you to do something, you never take it seriously. Jaya has brought photocopies of the representation and other documents. You just have to approve those—as simple as that.'

'It's not as easy as you think,' Bikash said, contradicting her. 'The state government can't make regular payments even to its permanent employees. How can I suggest a fresh recruitment at this time?'

'Have I ever asked you so strongly before to help any of my acquaintances? But Jaya is different. She is the only friend who is so close to me. Besides, her brother has a genuine claim on the job. He does not expect to become an officer; at best, he could get a clerk's job. I'm sure your department has provision for such appointments. But as usual, you are making excuses.' Itishree sounded restless and started fidgeting with the thick white envelope she held.

Bikash closed the magazine and looked at her. 'Okay, don't get so worked up,' he said. 'I've told you what the position is. It has become really difficult to manipulate such things. Put the envelope into my briefcase. Let me see what can be done.'

'What do you mean by "let me see"? You *must* get him the job,' Itishree said, opening his briefcase.

The next day, after Itishree had left for her college, Jaya called Bikash at his office at about twelve o'clock.

'Are you very busy?' she asked over the phone.

Bikash could not think of a quick reply. He had picked up the phone himself without thinking, as his PA was not in his cabin at the time.

'This is Jaya speaking; you probably couldn't place my voice.'

'No, no,' Bikash said defensively. 'I was just ...' He could not decide what to say.

'Iti has gone to her college. She said she has a lot of work today and won't be back before half past four. Why don't you come over for lunch? It is so boring to have lunch alone.'

'Sorry, but I'm ...' Bikash said hesitantly.

'Actually, I am feeling terribly bored alone. It'll be nice if you can make it. It'll take only a half hour. Please come,' Jaya pleaded.

'Okay, I am coming.' Bikash did not want to turn down the invitation to his own home.

The sound of the calling bell brought Jaya to her feet. She shook her hair loose and walked up to the front door. Bikash stood outside. Jaya greeted him with a charming smile and moved to one side to let him in.

'The cook has taken leave for an hour. He said he had some urgent work and I couldn't turn down his request. But we don't need him, do we?'

'It's all right,' Bikash said, feeling somewhat flustered.

Jaya served food for both of them. She sat across the table, facing Bikash, her face resting between her palms. 'Won't you have something?' Bikash asked, lowering the spoon he had lifted to his mouth.

Jaya smiled softly in reply. She raised her arms to gather up the masses of loose hair on her back and tied them into a bun. 'You finish first. I like to watch you eating. By the way, how do you like my cooking? Iti mentioned that you are fond of chow mein—so I made some for you.' Jaya said, looking relaxed and pleased with herself.

'I won't eat unless you do. You have to give me company,' Bikash insisted.

'All right, all right, I will eat—but you please carry on.'

'I've heard a lot about you,' Jaya said, raising her spoon.

'It couldn't be very complimentary,' Bikash remarked, looking straight at Jaya. He was beginning to feel relaxed.

'I have heard that you are a very capable officer, a person with very positive thinking, and a real intellectual.' Jaya chose each word with care. She locked her eyes with Bikash's and pressed her lips together to hold back a mischievous smile.

Once again, Jaya's hair had escaped the restraint of the knot that she had rolled it into and fallen across her back; once again, she lifted her arms, held the length of her hair, and began to tie it into a knot. She appeared quite relaxed and comfortable. Bikash's eyes were involuntarily drawn towards the bulge in Jaya's blouse that was partly revealed as she raised her arms. His face flushed scarlet and he began to turn the food on the plate with his spoon.

'You aren't saying anything,' Jaya persisted.

'I am none of the things you have described,' Bikash replied, looking into Jaya's eyes.

'Leave me to decide that. But please finish your food first.' She followed Bikash to the washbasin, towel in hand. Bikash's hand touched her fingers as he took the towel from Jaya. A shiver ran through him. Jaya's right hand reached out towards Bikash; there were a few cloves on the palm of her outstretched palm.

'Won't you rest for a while?' Jaya asked.

'I must rush back to the office. I have a meeting to attend,' Bikash answered, picking up two of the cloves she offered him.

'Please come again for lunch tomorrow—I will be waiting,' Jaya said, with the easy possessiveness of one who is mistress in her own house.

'I can't say for sure. I will try.'

'No, no—don't say you will try. You *have* to come, please! You must give me company, since Iti can't be here.' Jaya implored, smiling her most enchanting smile.

Bikash sat in his office but his thoughts were on Jaya. She is attractive; she has refined manners and a natural warmth about her. There was a wonderful touch of intimacy in her approach.

Her personality has something special, something magnetic that attracts people naturally. Bikash could see she was aware of her own appeal. He was not able to define the overpowering smell that her presence exuded. Jaya was an enigma.

Bikash wondered what all this would lead to. Let the inevitable happen, he thought resignedly.

On his way home from office, Bikash was apprehensive. He wondered if Jaya would have told Itishree about their secret rendezvous at lunchtime. He should have given Jaya a hint. His account and Jaya's of how they had spent the day must match, leaving no room for doubt in Iti's mind. But finally, he decided it would be wiser to keep quiet.

'What did you do all day?' Iti asked, looking at Jaya. 'You must have been bored stiff! Too bad I couldn't keep you company; the pressure of work in the college has increased so much these days. The exams are going on and taking leave has become a problem.' She sounded apologetic.

'You mustn't look so guilty,' Jaya said. 'Actually, I quite enjoyed the day. It's not always that I am able to relax in this way. I had a good lunch, listened to music, watched television, and had a great time.' Jaya replied. Bikash heard her, let out a breath of relief, and returned his attention to the newspaper he was leafing through.

Next day, exactly at one o'clock, Jaya called Bikash at his office.

'Have you finished your work for the morning? I have prepared lunch for you myself. Come soon, I'll be waiting.'

'Okay,' Bikash said shortly. He couldn't think of anything more to say.

As on the day before, Jaya opened the door, smiling her welcome smile, and as she did so, she gathered up the hair hanging loose on her back and rolled it into a bun. She dished out the food for both of them and sat at the table facing Bikash. The air around her was permeated with that overpowering smell. It agitated him.

'You have to tell me if you like my cooking. I have cooked this mushroom myself,' Jaya said.

'It is excellent,' Bikash replied with a smile.

'Oh, how forgetful of me—I have left the bottle of mineral water in the kitchen.' She got up from her chair and moved towards the kitchen. 'The cook wanted to go for a movie. I gave him leave to go,' she said, turning at the door of the kitchen. Her hair had again slid down her back. Once again, the familiar strong smell floated up to Bikash. He cast a quick glance at his watch. It was almost two o'clock.

'Come, Bikash,' Jaya said and immediately thrust out her tongue between her teeth, in the familiar gesture that women in India make to indicate a slip of the tongue. 'I am sorry—Bikash Babu, I should have said! Shall we listen to some music?'

'You can always call me Bikash,' Bikash said huskily.

'Fine, Bikash then! Come, take a little rest now.' Bikash followed Jaya to his own bedroom.

'What kind of music should I play for you?' she asked, standing in front of the music system. Bikash stood close behind her. As Jaya was about to insert a CD into the music player, Bikash pressed her palm lightly. Without turning, leaning sideways gently against Bikash, she craned her neck slightly to let her head rest on his right shoulder. She looked up at Bikash, a knowing smile on her lips. Bikash wound his hands tightly around Jaya's waist and drew her closer. She lifted her left arm and, locking it around Bikash's neck, slung herself against him, standing on her toes. Without wasting a moment, Bikash crushed Jaya's lips under his and, pushing the sari off her shoulder, thrust an impatient hand inside her blouse....

'What are we going to do tomorrow? Iti says she will be back by two o'clock,' Jaya asked Bikash as he prepared to leave for the office after half an hour. Bikash couldn't think at once of a solution to the problem Jaya had raised.

'Take a room in some hotel,' Jaya said. 'We shall have lunch there. Send the car by one o'clock. I will tell Iti that I have to go and meet my aunt who lives in Cuttack,' Jaya suggested promptly.

'Fine, I will do that,' Bikash said. It was nearly three in the afternoon. He left for the office in a hurry.

He returned late that evening. Before he stepped inside, Itishree came to him with her complaint.

'You are late, Bikash! You could have accompanied us to the market if you had come earlier.'

'Iti bought this sari for me though I insisted she shouldn't,' Jaya said. The statement was meant for Bikash.

'So, what was the big deal?' Itishree broke in. 'We have met after such a long time! We could have had dinner out if he had come a little earlier. But as you can see, he is never serious about such things.'

Jaya smiled her enigmatic smile, looking at no one in particular.

'Well, you didn't come shopping with us, nor could you find time to take us out for dinner! But all that will be forgiven, provided you do something to help her out with her problem!' Itishree said to her husband later that night as they were about to go to bed. There was no reply from Bikash.

'You aren't even listening!' she complained. 'What have you done about it?'

'Oh, can't you let a man sleep?' Bikash said, exasperated. 'Haven't I told you that I am trying? I have asked for the file to be put up.'

Itishree muttered something and turned over on her side.

∾

Bikash had booked a suite at Hotel Namrata as planned. He sent his car to pick up Jaya and drop her at the hotel.

Around half past three in the afternoon, as they were checking out, Bikash handed Jaya an envelope.

'What is this?' Jaya asked.

'Open it and see for yourself,' Bikash answered.

With impatient hands, Jaya tore the envelope open and pulled out the official document, neatly folded four times. She smoothed it out and began to read. Her eyes sparkled as they travelled over the lines.

'Oh, how wonderful!' she exclaimed excitedly. 'I can't believe it! So quick! You are really a wizard, Bikash!' She looked at him, her eyes wide open in surprise and admiration. The next moment, she put the letter and the envelope on the table and embraced Bikash.

'You are exceptionally efficient!' Jaya said adoringly.

'Okay,' Bikash said with a smile, 'Keep that letter carefully, and hurry up. It's time we checked out.'

Jaya folded the letter, put it in the envelope, and handed it back to Bikash.

'Let the letter be with you. I am returning to Rourkela tonight. That letter will give me an excuse to come back here and stay for a few days. Does that suit you?' Jaya asked, a smile dancing on her lips.

'How incredibly clever!' Bikash exclaimed and kissed Jaya once again.

As he was leaving for the office the following day, Bikash turned at the gate to look back. Both Itishree and Jaya stood at the gate. Itishree looked a little anxious but Jaya stood smiling her special secret smile.

'You must return early,' Itishree said. 'We have to see Jaya off at the station.' She turned to Jaya and said, 'He is so forgetful he will forget you are leaving today if he isn't reminded.' The two friends went inside and closed the door. Itishree had taken leave for the day.

തൠ

'Jaya, don't worry. I shall not give him a moment's rest until your work is done! Bikash says it will take just a few days.'

All three were standing on the platform, waiting for the train to arrive.

'Yes, keep reminding him at intervals,' Jaya said. 'I shall be in touch.'

'Do you have to tell me that? But you must call me and try to come here whenever you have the time. Jeetu's birthday is in August. You must come!'

'I promise!'

The train arrived. Slowly, Jaya released her hands from Itishree's grip and, joining her palms together, touched them to her forehead. 'Namaskar,' she said to Bikash and got into the compartment. The guard blew his whistle and the train began to roll out of the platform. Standing at the door, Jaya waved at Bikash and Itishree.

A Real Diamond!

The driver parked the car in the porch. Sikta got off, opened the front door, and entered the house. The driver took out the suitcase from the car and put it down on the floor. He stood waiting for further orders.

'Sahib will come tomorrow. You can go now. Come tomorrow,' Sikta told him.

'I'll take the car to the airport to receive him, ma'am,' the driver said. He touched his finger to his forehead in a polite salute and left. Sikta knew there would be nobody at home at that hour. Neither the cook nor the gardener was aware that she was coming back from Ranchi that day. It was not yet time for the cleaning maid to come. She would have an hour to herself.

She had grown accustomed long ago to the solitude of her home.

She felt like a stranger each time she looked at its lavish furnishings, the expensive paintings on the walls, the thick rugs on the floor, or the garden with its ornate lights and elegant granite statues, specially ordered from Puri. She wondered why the house that bore the mark of her own impeccable taste should make her feel so unsure of herself, as if she was an outsider here.

Why indeed?

Why did a shadow of impermanence hang over everything? It was not easy to define exactly what she missed but there was a constant longing to return where she actually belonged. But she was not sure where it was. She also knew that it was a vain hope that she nurtured. She should have had no complaint against life. In fact, she argued with herself, life had given her much more than she had hoped for. The beautiful house that looked as though it was straight out of a picture postcard, surpassed all the enchanting pictures that her imagination could have conjured up.

In spite of that, the memory of the house where she had spent her childhood would not leave her. The house, with its spreading garden, surrounded by paddy fields that stretched unendingly to the horizon, was like a magic wand that unveiled a new panorama of dreams each day.

But the enchantment was not destined to last long.

Her father was transferred to Bhubaneswar shortly afterwards and they had to shift to a flat on the upper floor of a block of four apartments. Two small bedrooms, a tiny sitting room, and a miniature balcony enclosed by an iron grill completed the set-up.

'It's like a match-box,' Mother grumbled. 'We were fated to live in this cage after five years in that sprawling house!' she said unhappily, without accusing anyone in particular. Sikta felt equally disappointed in the beginning. It appeared as if she had been thrown out of a dream world to land in that tiny apartment suspended in mid-air.

The filthy courtyard of the occupants of the lower flat, with the feminine undergarments hanging unabashedly from a plastic clothesline, caught the eye immediately when one looked down through the balcony at the rear. The flat opposite was a replica of their own. Behind the fluttering curtain in the window that faced the balcony, an elusive, curious face that could be anyone's—a young boy's or an adult's or a woman's sometimes. In the front, there was the wide street, chaotic with the rumble of constantly moving traffic, save for a few hours of quietude in the night.

It was the large garden, with its abundance of fruit trees and flowering plants, and the vast open field beyond it, serving as a playground, that Sikta missed the most. But here, there was only the flight of concrete stairs that led to the terrace, which was shared by all the families. She had fit her wandering fancies into that limited space. She tried to discover a time when the terrace would be empty but it was not easy. She had to go to school, cope with the increasing pressure of studies, and spend time with the friends she had just made. It was only in the afternoons that she found time for herself. The girls in that block of flats preferred to sit and gossip on the culvert in front than to go up to the terrace. Sometimes, her mother came with her but she was mostly alone. Instead of peering down at the scene below, Sikta chose to sit down. Then the busy world outside was shut out; the dingy courtyard and the vehicles on the street below were hidden away and there was only the endless stretch of the sky above. Patches of white cloud, soft like her own youthful dreams, sailed across it.

Perhaps there was some special power in her that could help discover the magic hidden in drabness around her. Everything bewitched her young heart.

It was not the same now.

She could no longer feel one with nature. She was immune to the magic of moonlit nights, the mystery of the star-spangled night sky, or the tingle of unexpected rain. What had taken the magic away? Was it time? Why couldn't she feel the same overwhelming joy now, although she knew that she had no binding engagements that could have stopped her from indulging her fancies?

It might be because of the absence of Amar, her husband. She tried to imagine how many times the joy could have been multiplied had Amar been there to share her moments of ecstasy. Sikta understood that she was in that special phase of life when the heart yearns for the company of a loved one.

Her trip to Ranchi and her meeting with the sadhu baba had been a unique experience. She had been a little dubious at first. It would be her first night out alone and she felt slightly insecure. But the meeting turned out to be a memorable event. She could not find words to describe the experience. Others might call it a hallucination but she knew it was almost a tangible reality.

The sadhu baba asked her to close her eyes. She did not remember how long she remained with eyes shut. She had perhaps gone into a trance. She seemed to be wandering in another land, in another time. The moonlight bathed everything in a silvery glow. A soft, cool breeze was blowing. There was no one around. She felt herself to be floating in the air, her body weightless. Suddenly, her eyes fell on a white crystalline rock that glimmered like silver. Even as she watched, it began to melt slowly, until nothing was left of it, and in its place stood a woman. Sikta looked closely at the figure.

It was she herself!

The silver rock had metamorphosed into a woman who was none other than Sikta!

Her eyes opened. The sadhu baba was standing before her, his face lit up by an ethereal glow. The air around was permeated with an unknown fragrance.

'What did you see?' he asked her.

'I saw ...' She could not speak. Her eyes brimmed with unshed tears. 'The rock changed into a woman. Who was she? Was it I?'

The sadhu baba did not say anything. Nor did his face register any change of expression. Sikta waited for some time and finally returned.

All through her journey from Ranchi back home, a question tormented her. What was the meaning of that unusual vision? She had left nearly half of her life behind and had reached a point where she had developed a detachment towards a lot of things. Did it mean that there was a different kind of life awaiting her? Or was she about to unravel the truth that had evaded her all these years? She kept brooding until she reached home.

And now, she turned her eyes around and looked at the elegant furnishings in her home—the mahogany sofa set, the huge twin mirrors in the drawing room that faced each other, as if they had been engraved into the walls, the Ravi Varma paintings, the tinted glass panels fitted in the windows, and the cut-glass chandelier that hung from the ceiling. All of them were like living members of her family. They shared her joys and sorrows and were mute witness to all her emotional swings.

The clatter of utensils in the kitchen roused Sikta from reverie. The cook had perhaps got news of her return. Sikta was not hungry, nor was she inclined any longer to let her life fall into a regular pattern. She opened the door of the drawing room and walked up to the iron grill that enclosed the veranda. The creepers of *radha tamal*, which had been her favourite flowers, clung to the grill. Surprisingly, she had never tried to know the name of the beautiful dark blue, wheel-shaped flowers that bloomed and withered away after having filled the air with their delicate fragrance for a small time.

Sikta opened the grill door and stepped out into the garden. It was as if she was looking at her own garden for the first time.

The gardener tended the plants with great care. The small, neatly mowed patch of grass, as soft as a carpet, with varieties of flowers growing around it, resembled a toy garden. Sikta realized now that she had never allowed herself to experience the joy which proximity to her favourite flowers could have given her. Instead, she had kept yearning for Amar's company. That precious 'something' which could have filled the void within her had been just within her reach, but she had wasted a lot of time in its quest.

She asked the gardener to put out a portable table and a few chairs under the *ashoka* tree. Then she asked the cook to bring her a cup of tea. As she settled in the garden chair, her eyes fell on a woman who was standing near the gate. She looked like Trishna Bose, wife of Samir Bose, a high-ranking executive in the steel company. Sikta remembered meeting her at some party. Trishna Bose was an amiable person with a good sense of humour, some five years younger than her.

She used to phone Sikta and visit her occasionally, but Sikta never felt inclined to return her visits. She found it difficult to maintain such formalities, though she could be a good enough hostess.

As the woman came closer, Sikta had a clear view of her. Yes, it was Trishna Bose.

'Namaskar, Didi,' Trishna said smiling at her. 'Why are you sitting here alone?'

'It's very peaceful here. Come, have a seat,' Sikta said. She called the gardener and asked him to tell the cook to bring two more cups of tea along with some biscuits.

'Isn't Bhai Sahib at home?' Trishna asked.

'No, he hasn't returned from Singapore yet.'

'I must say Bhai Sahib is a gem of a man—a diamond, I call him!' Trishna said admiringly. 'My husband says he has the Midas touch. Any business he lays his hand on becomes gold!'

Trishna's words had no effect on Sikta. The cook came carrying the cups of tea and a plate of biscuits on a tray and placed it on the table. She handed a cup to Trishna and glanced at her. She did not want to say anything, yet the words gushed out of her without warning. 'All that *I* had wanted was a handful of earth in which I could have sowed a wish and watched it grow into a tree!'

She spoke if in a trance—the words imprisoned in some secluded region of her heart finding a sudden release.

Trishna Bose looked at her with embarrassment. The outburst of emotion had taken her by surprise. Sikta controlled herself. Why did she have to say all this to Trishna? Could she understand?

'Sorry!' she said. 'I said all that because you called him a diamond.' She tried to wipe away the seriousness with her smile. 'Diamond indeed!' she continued. 'See, I'm wearing a diamond on my finger. Look, how it dazzles. I show it to everybody. It is such a precious thing that I can't take it off my finger for fear of losing it!' Sikta was still smiling.

Trishna sipped her tea without uttering a word, staring into her teacup. Sikta felt sorry for Trishna. Poor girl! She had come to visit her, all dressed up for the occasion, and Sikta had embarrassed her. She did not deserve this!

'I'll take leave now, Didi,' Trishna said, rising to her feet. 'I'll come some other day.' Sikta knew well that she would not come again.

'Come, let me walk you to the gate,' Sikta said and stood up.

Jungle Lore

It was one o'clock in the afternoon by the time they arrived at the forest guest house. They had started at six in the morning and stopped briefly at Chainbasa for tea and snacks. After Chainbasa, the road ran through the jungle. The ride, though bumpy, had its own charm. Prachi enjoyed the solitude and closeness to nature. The tall trees as well as the shrubs and creepers on both flanks of the road appeared to be moving ahead in step with them as the Land Rover roared and bumped along the uneven track that cut through the jungle. Beautiful birds of different breeds filled the air with their chirping. The meandering rivulets of River Karo met them at different bends as the vehicle negotiated the curves in the track. Prachi was fascinated by the exotic smell of winter flowers and the fragrance of wild jasmine that permeated the atmosphere. Time and again, they stopped to take pictures.

The landscape changed as they entered the forest of Saranda. The forest grew denser and it became difficult to see things more than a few feet ahead. One of the two Land Rovers they travelled in carried their luggage. The cook and the helping hands had gone ahead the day before with the provisions and camping equipment. A couple of tents were pitched in front of the guest house and a coarse *satranji* had been spread out, where half a dozen plastic chairs stood awaiting their weary bodies.

As they moved on, Prachi recollected the day her life had changed.

It had happened just ten days ago, on the 24th. Prachi remembered the day and time clearly—it was a Friday afternoon. She had entered Sambit's chamber carrying a file. He seemed a little absent-minded and did not notice her presence for a time.

'Sir,' Prachi called. Sambit turned to look but his gaze seemed to be fixed on something behind her. With a conscious effort, she resisted turning her head to find out what it was that Sambit was looking at.

'Have a seat,' he said. Prachi lowered herself into a chair. Sambit did not speak for quite a while. He leafed through the pages of the file silently. She knew that the file contained important matters and needed to be disposed of urgently. But Sambit's mind seemed to be elsewhere.

'I have to tell you something,' Sambit said at last, looking straight into her eyes.

Prachi continued to sit quietly, looking at him questioningly.

'I want to marry you.' Sambit's voice was clear and confident.

Prachi looked at him wide-eyed in astonishment and shock. The suddenness of the proposition had thrown her off balance.

'What are you thinking?' he asked with a smile. 'Perhaps you would want a little time to decide?' He was speaking with ease now and seemed to be enjoying Prachi's embarrassment.

Prachi fumbled. A few disjointed words escaped inadvertently. 'My parents .... I am not sure ...'

'Okay, I will ask my mom and dad to meet your parents today. But keep it secret for the time being. And now,' Sambit said in his professional voice, 'let's get back to work, right?' Prachi nodded weakly and followed him out of the room.

She was flummoxed at the unexpected development of events. It was a totally new experience for her. A man, and a gentleman at that, asking for her hand! How should she have reacted? What had happened a few minutes earlier did not seem to fit into any pattern. She had no idea what the appropriate atmosphere should have been for broaching such a subject. Her thoughts regarding her own marriage had not yet acquired a shape; marriage was a mysterious territory to her, which she had never dared to venture into in her thoughts.

Sambit and his parents came to meet her father and mother. They said they were proud of their son's choice and gave their consent to the marriage happily. Her own parents too were delighted. They thought Sambit would be a perfect match for their daughter. The wedding ceremony was tentatively scheduled for April.

Within no time, the news spread through the office. The excitement of their colleagues as they came to know about it exceeded the joy of Prachi's parents and her own bewilderment. There were six engineers, including Sambit, working for that unit of the steel multinational company. Prachi was one of the seven research assistants who worked under them. Everyone came up to Prachi to congratulate her. They forced her to come into Sambit's chamber during the lunch break. Several packets of sweets lay open on the table. The entire lunch break passed in eating and feeding sweets to one another and jubilation over the exciting news.

That day, when they were alone, Sambit asked Prachi to apply for leave until the engagement ceremony was over. It wouldn't look proper for her to work in the office as his junior any longer, he said solicitously. His family was not in favour of Prachi's continuing to work. She should resign as soon as possible. Sambit suggested she should give the office notice next month of her intention to quit. Prachi, too, did not have much interest in the job.

'What are you thinking so deeply, Prachi?' Pragnya, who had been observing Prachi's absent-mindedness, asked. 'We know what thoughts must be passing through your mind,' she remarked playfully.

Sambit turned in his seat to look at them, his lips curved in a mischievous smile. It was quite natural that she should be dreaming about their marriage. The jeep pulled up in front of the guest house. Sambit reached out to hold Prachi's hand and helped her climb down. A shiver ran through her body at his touch. She liked the caring gesture.

'Prachi, have you put on full shoes? The jungle is full of thorny bushes!' Sambit asked with concern, looking down at Prachi's feet.

Prachi wore a pair of jeans, a white T-shirt, and full shoes, as Sambit had advised her. She sensed Sambit's eyes surveying her as they started the journey.

'The thorns will be specially attracted to Prachi; they won't be interested in us!' Pragnya remarked teasingly and broke into laughter. Prachi's face flushed red. A shy smile ran over Sambit's lips.

The table was set for pre-lunch drinks. Bottles of beer packed in ice boxes were placed on the table. Soft drinks were served to the girls. Freshly fried chicken pakora arrived to go with the drinks. The three men in the group raised their beer mugs. 'Cheers!' they said. Sambit turned to look at Prachi. 'A toast to my fiancée, with her permission!' he proposed, and touched the mug to his lips. Prachi smiled a little. Others clapped. 'Hereafter, Sambit will require permission for anything he does!' Avinash, Sambit's friend and colleague, teased him. There was another roar of laughter. The air was thick with the aroma of meat and potatoes being cooked into a spicy curry. It would take some more time to get lunch ready. The drinks and the chicken pakora had taken care of their appetite for the time being.

'Let's take a walk in the jungle,' someone suggested. Others agreed immediately. A local lad, with a big canvas bag slung over his shoulder, walked ahead. They chatted noisily as they walked. Sambit was by Prachi's side all the time. It was a delectable experience for her. The atmosphere seemed to be full of the promise of love.

A rustling sound came from somewhere close by. It was followed by a soft hiss. Everyone stopped abruptly. They strained their ears to listen but could not identify the sound. Could it be some wild animal? Fear gripped Prachi's heart. Sambit moved closer to her and held her hand tightly.

'Oh my God!' Pragnya let out a scream and, leaping a foot or so into the air, landed at the spot where Sambit and Prachi stood. It happened suddenly, before others could see or understand anything. She was trembling uncontrollably. Her lips moved but no word came. The other five followed her gaze. The sight was terrifying enough to turn them to stone. Slightly ahead, to the right, was a bamboo clump and, coiled around the foot of one of the thick bamboo plants, which leant out a little, was an enormous python. Its eyes blazed in anger and a loud hissing sound came from its slightly open jaws. Sambit put his finger to his lips, warning the others not to make a noise. They stood rooted to the ground as if under a spell, their eyes fixed on the awe-inspiring yet beautiful creature. Slowly, the snake drew its head back and turned it in the opposite direction. The hissing sound decreased. As the python began to inch out of the clump, its huge length, which had been coiled around the bamboo plant, was revealed slowly and it slithered into the depths of the jungle. It took more than ten minutes for the snake to move out of sight.

'You know, the force of the snake's breath practically lifted me off the ground!' Pragnya exclaimed. She was regaining control over herself. 'Oh, I have sprained my leg!' she groaned and slumped on the ground. She took out a tube of balm from the first-aid kit and applied it to her ankle.

'We should have fired a shot or two at it to scare it away, instead of standing like statues! It would have been fun, wouldn't it?' Avinash remarked.

'It would be most unwise!' Sambit said. 'It was a deadly creature. Its reaction to the firing would be quite unpredictable. We're lucky it went away of its own accord without causing any harm to anyone. It is rash to challenge such wild creatures,' Sambit explained to his friends.

'We have come far enough into the jungle,' Prachi said, looking at Sambit. 'Let's go back.'

'There's no need to feel worried when I'm around,' Sambit said. 'I'm quite used to wild animals and know how to handle them. There will be more of them as we go further. It's an experience that shouldn't be missed.'

True, thought Prachi. There might be many more surprises in store ahead. They walked on.

After they had walked for a half hour, a clearing in the jungle came into sight. Pragnya sat down, holding her injured foot. 'I can't walk anymore,' she moaned. Their guide spread out a satranji on the ground and the three girls sat down. Leaving the boy with them, the three young men moved ahead.

'Prachi didi, please tell us your love story. Was it you or Sambit bhai that made the first declaration of love?' Suparna, the youngest of the girls, asked Prachi, her face glowing with curiosity. Prachi was silent for a moment. She couldn't remember any such thing happening to her. The wedding was still six months away. Romance may come with growing intimacy—she smiled as she thought about it.

'It's not enough to give us that coy smile!' Pragnya joined Suparna. 'You've got to tell us everything.'

'It came to me as a big surprise too,' said Prachi haltingly. 'It was so sudden!'

'Yes, it surprised everyone! We were expecting Sambit bhai to propose to Apurba didi ...,' Pragnya blurted out. There was an awkward silence for a few moments, as if someone had unwittingly let a skeleton out of a closet.

'It's a pity Apurba didi didn't join us,' Suparna said, breaking the silence. 'She's such fun!' She was watching Prachi's face intently. They saw the three young men walking towards them, their faces shining with sweat and excitement.

Sambit came up to Prachi. 'Quick, come with us and be careful not to make a sound,' he said to her in a hoarse, urgent whisper, taking her hand and helping her to her feet. He motioned to the boy to follow them and almost pulled Prachi along with him. 'Quick!' he urged again. They strode on for more than five minutes to reach the spot where Sambit wanted to take them. Prachi was filled with excitement at what she saw. It was a magical sight. A flock of peacocks, unaware of their presence, strutted around majestically without fear. The hens darted here and there while the peacocks, raising their lovely plumes, kept running and hopping in joy. Prachi had never seen such a thing before. Her heart leapt with joy. Unaware of what she was doing, she caught hold of Sambit's right hand with both of hers and pressed it hard. Sambit disengaged his hand from Prachi's grip and went back a few steps. He returned almost immediately, a shotgun in his hand. Prachi guessed instantly what was going to happen. Her eyes grew wide with terror. Before she could say anything, Sambit's left hand went round her neck and his palm pressed down firmly over her mouth. She stood there numb with fear, held captive in Sambit's grip, unable to utter a word. Sambit pulled her down to a sitting position and sat down on his knees by her side.

'We had a bet. I have accepted their challenge to fell three of the birds with a single shot,' he whispered into her ear.

Prachi continued to stare in horror at the beautiful birds moving about happily, unaware of the danger. Sambit took aim and squeezed the trigger. Prachi shut her eyes. The shot boomed out, and a brief silence followed; and then the air was filled with the agonized screams of the three peahens that lay writhing on the ground. The other birds in the flock screeched loudly and ran blindly in different directions, their cries of terror resonating through the jungle. Prachi opened her eyes and saw the three peahens lying on the forest floor, flapping their wings in a horrible death agony. Prachi was reminded of the Founder's Day celebration that had taken place at the steel factory a few years ago. There was a big crowd in the carnival ground. For some unknown reason, the police fired a couple of blank shots in the air and people ran helter-skelter, turning the carnival into bedlam. Sambit released Prachi and got to his feet, a triumphant glow on his face. Pragnya and Avinash ran to see the peahens. 'Hurrah! Three with one shot! Bravo, Sambit bhai!' Pragnya shouted excitedly. 'You have won,' Avinash announced, his voice filled with admiration. 'But what are we going to do with these dead birds? I'm told some people eat peacock meat. Let's take them back with us and give them to the cook.'

'No,' Sambit advised. 'Peacock meat isn't tasty at all; it's fibrous and rubbery. Let us leave them for the wolves.'

'We have had enough excitement, let's return,' Avinash said and they started back towards the guest house.

'Won't there be a problem?' Pragnya asked, turning to look at the dead birds. 'There is a ban on hunting, isn't there?'

'Don't worry,' Sambit assured her. 'The forest guards are known to us. I've been here with my dad a number of times. There will be no trace of the birds by evening.'

After ten minutes or so, they reached a spot where a narrow track branched out to the right and entered the jungle. 'You all can go ahead,' Sambit said, 'Prachi and I shall go this way and have a look at the stream.' He caught hold of Prachi's hand and led her to the track.

'Okay, okay,' Pragnya said with a knowing smile. The other moved on, leaving Sambit and Prachi together.

'I haven't had a chance to be alone with you for the last ten days,' Sambit said. 'There's so much I want to talk to you about!' They walked together along that deserted track. Prachi looked up at him. 'Do you know why I chose you to marry?' he said. Prachi waited. 'It is because of your soft nature. A wife should be mild and able to adapt to all kinds of situations, because ultimately, it is she who has to shoulder the family responsibilities. We both belong to respectable families. Why should my wife have to work as long as I am able to take care of the needs of the family? I am glad you and your family accepted my suggestion.' Sambit paused. He looked genuinely relieved because he had been able to unburden himself of his thoughts. Prachi gazed fixedly at the stream that came down from the mountain and flowed through the jungle, making a low, lapping sound. The silence of the forest lent it an enigmatic charm. She drank in the beauty of the scene thirstily.

'You are so beautiful!' Sambit whispered in her ear. He put his hand on her shoulder and gently turned her to face him. 'I've been hoping and waiting for this moment!' Before she could think of something to say, the strong smell of beer assaulted her nostrils, and the next moment, she felt Sambit's lips pressing down on her own.

Does the first experience have to be like this? Prachi wondered. Is this the shoulder that will support and guide me through the journey of life? She was feeling a little unsure.

They sat down on two rocks that stood close to each other. Both were silent, absorbed in their own thoughts. Prachi fidgeted unmindfully with a bunch of wild jasmine.

'Hey, there is something on your mind. Tell me, what is it?' Sambit asked, watching her intently.

'Apurba didi—' The words spurted out of her unwilling lips.

'Oh, Apurba!' Sambit replied carelessly. 'She was just a good friend. I would never have married such a haughty girl, who claims an equal status with men. They are all right as friends, but they can never make good wives.

'I must be frank with you, Prachi,' he continued. 'I would like you to be like my mother. I will try to fulfil all your wishes, but in return, I would expect you to adapt yourself to the lifestyle of my family. I would like you to be the perfect wife and homemaker.' He held her arms lovingly and raised her to her feet. 'Let's get back to our friends. They must be waiting for us.' As Prachi took a step forward, Sambit turned abruptly and locked her in his arms. 'Please, darling, one more kiss!' he begged. Once more, the smell of beer stung her nostrils. Prachi turned and cast one last look at the stream that flowed gaily through the jungle.

'I am the one who is doing all the talking,' Sambit complained fondly. 'Don't you have anything to say about our marriage?'

'I love to hear you speak,' Prachi said and smiled softly.

Hand in hand, they walked back to the tent. By the time they had washed their hands, steaming hot rice and aromatic meat curry had been served. All of them began to eat hungrily.

'Prachi is just nibbling at her food. What is the matter? Has Sambit bhai cast some spell on you?' Pragnya teased her.

'That's exactly what I was going to say. I can understand if Sambit has no appetite left, but Prachi ...' Once again, a roar of laughter filled the air.

Daylight was fading. They prepared to return. The coming of night is a special phenomenon in a forest. Day and night meet intimately to welcome and bid farewell to each other. The viewer cannot help marvelling at the seamless blending of light and darkness. He feels that he is the only witness to this union. It was a strange kind of experience, Prachi reflected as she watched the evening sneaking into the jungle.

The two Land Rovers rolled along the bumpy jungle path. Pragnya and Avinash began humming a tune. Sambit joined them, trying to catch up with the refrain. The vehicles came out of the jungle and moved up the hilly road. Sambit motioned the driver of the jeep behind theirs to stop. He brought the Land Rover he himself was driving to a stop and climbed down. 'Get down, all of you,' he said. 'Let's bid farewell to the jungle!'

'Goodbye!' They yelled in chorus.

'Say something, Prachi,' Sambit said, with a soft, intimate glance at her. 'I am so happy today that I would like to give you a gift! What should I give you? Tell me … anything you want.'

They all crowded around Prachi. Pragnya came closer and spoke in her ear, in a low whisper that Sambit could not hear. 'Don't let go of such a golden opportunity,' she said, trying to sound conspiratorial. 'Ask for something solid—I would suggest a beautiful diamond ring.'

Prachi did not say anything.

'Come on … anything, Prachi, anything. Tell me what you want,' Sambit repeated.

Prachi glanced at him for a moment and turned to face the jungle. She shut her eyes. Pictures of the greenery of the jungle, the yellow-winged butterflies hovering over the forest flowers, and the hissing python floated up before her closed eyes. There was a strong, unfamiliar smell in the air. Was it the beer? Or was it that special smell of a winter evening settling over the forest? Prachi was not able to define it. She inhaled deeply, trying to identify the smell. The exotic fragrance of the forest flowers was mingled with another strange smell.

And then she knew! It was the smell of blood!

Her eyes jerked open as the truth hit her with stunning force. She no longer felt unsure of herself. 'The three peahens! Can you give them to me—alive?'

A Fable for the Times

'Let there be free food for all my people!'

'Open the royal treasuries and give away all the royal gems to the poor!'

'Distribute my garments of silk and velvet among my subjects!'

'Stop the war against the rebels! Let there be peace!'

The royal couple had been blessed with a baby girl at last after living through the curse of childlessness for long years. Great was the people's rejoicing. The king's subjects celebrated the royal birth with unprecedented pomp, the cares of daily life forgotten. Crowds thronged the royal palace to catch a glimpse of the little princess, whose beauty surpassed the radiance of the moon.

The royal priest chanted mantras while the royal astrologer was busy charting the positions of the planets at the moment of her birth and drawing up her horoscope. 'The princess has been born under the most auspicious stars,' the astrologer declared, 'and will bring good fortune to her husband as well as her parents.' The baby was named Sujasha, which means 'one who has been blessed with fame'. The royal couple felt elated.

But suddenly, the astrologer's face grew dark with apprehension as he continued to study the position of the planets. Lines of worry appeared on his forehead. His consternation was immediately transferred to the king and the queen.

'What is it?' asked the king anxiously.

'Oh my God! What is the matter now?' A soft scream escaped the queen's mouth.

After a long pause, the astrologer said, 'Your Majesties, this is the most extraordinary horoscope I have ever cast or seen. The combination of stars and planets is most strange. The horoscope shows a negative planetary influence over the sixth house, which is the house of love, producing a juxtaposition of worldliness and spirituality in the subject. There is a possibility that the princess may renounce all worldly attachments and become a *sannyasin* when she grows up.'

'Renounce the world!' The queen was startled. The courtiers who were watching turned pale.

'Such a fate would bring ruin to any kingdom!' the king said, deep in thought. 'She is a princess—no ordinary mortal. One day, she will marry a prince and adorn her husband's palace. She will bear the heir to the throne. The queen has to be mother not only to her own children but also to every one of her subjects. And, most important of all, she will be expected to live a life of luxury and grandeur, as befits a princess. How can the future queen renounce the world?'

'I admit, Your Majesty, that this is most unusual. I am confused!' the astrologer said.

'Find some means to prevent it then!' the king ordered.

'I will try, Your Majesty!' the astrologer said. 'I implore you to be patient.'

The celebration that had been stopped for a while was resumed. The dancing and music started again.

While the palace throbbed with jubilation, something exciting was happening in the royal stables, where the king's horses were kept. The most beautiful and swift of all the horses in the stable was a mare named Mallika, who had just given birth to a healthy and lovable filly. It was brown in colour and had a triangular white patch on its forehead. Its hooves were white. The eyes of the chief stable-keeper, Banamali, sparkled with joy. The king, who was a great lover of horses, would be delighted by the arrival of this beautiful foal, which was female too, and would, in time, rival its mother in grace, beauty, and speed.

What might be an appropriate name for such a beautiful creature? Banamali couldn't think of one. He would have rushed to the king with the happy news had it been some other time and begged the king to step into the stable to have a look at Mallika's newborn baby and give it a name. But today was a special day. The entire kingdom was bubbling with excitement. There were celebrations everywhere. A new princess had been born. How could Banamali trouble the king with news of a filly's birth at a time like this?

The foal staggered to a standing position as Banamali watched it fondly, but almost immediately, its legs sagged and it fell. The little legs were not yet strong enough to hold up its small body. He allowed the filly to continue with its efforts to stand up and did nothing to interfere. After a few more attempts, the foal stood up, although unsteadily. Mallika watched the struggles of her baby. Then she moved her hind legs apart to make room for the baby. The filly sniffed its way to its mother's teats and began to suckle.

For Banamali, the incident was just a repetition of something that occurred every other day in the stables.

Nevertheless, he was thrilled. He marvelled at the miracle of birth. An overwhelming sense of gratitude urged him to join his palms in gratitude to the Creator.

'Sarita!' he said and stroked the back of the newborn filly lovingly. 'That is the name you will be called by! You will grow up to become a strong and swift mare, since you have been born on a very auspicious day, the same day on which our princess has been born.' Banamali talked to the filly for a few moments and rose to his feet. He had to get some nutritious food for Mallika.

Princess Sujasha grew up to become as radiant as the moon in its bright phase; the palace was lit up by her beauty. The plants in the royal garden that would otherwise have appeared dull and lifeless took on a lush look. Deer sported in the royal forests and birds sang melodiously in the trees. The little princess played happily with them. She fed peacocks with her own hands. She stood quietly by the hibiscus plants in the royal gardens, caressing the bright red flowers. But what she liked best was the lake inside the garden, with its crystal-clear waters and hundreds of lotus flowers blooming in it. It was there that she had learnt to swim as a child.

Then, one bright morning ...

Princess Sujasha, having bathed in the lake, was strolling through the royal gardens with a newly opened lotus bud in her hand, accompanied by her maids. Suddenly, a young mare from the royal stables galloped past her.

'A new mare?' the princess exclaimed in surprise. 'I have never seen her before!'

'Haven't you, Your Royal Highness?' one of the maids said. 'She is the most beautiful and swiftest of all the animals in the royal stables. Her name is Sarita.'

A breathless Banamali ran up to them just then. 'I pray to God that Your Royal Highness hasn't been hurt,' he said with concern. 'Sarita has become so playful that we were not able to restrain her.'

'They tell me she is the most swift and strong of all the horses in the royal stables,' Princess Sujasha said. 'How old is she?'

'She was born on the same day as yourself, Royal Highness,' Banamali answered.

'Really!' The lovely face of the princess lit up with excitement. 'Then I must ride this mare. You must teach me to ride,' Princess Sujasha said.

'But you are too young to ride a horse, Your Royal Highness!' Banamali said. 'You will certainly learn horse riding after a few more years.'

'No, I want to begin now!' the princess said, stamping her feet impatiently.

'His Majesty may not approve of it!' Banamali said, trying to dissuade the princess.

'Then we won't let him know,' the princess said, her eyes sparkling with mischief.

Sarita had trotted up to the place where the princess and Banamali were speaking to each other. The young mare stood quietly with her head lowered.

'Isn't she supposed to be the most docile of the horses in the royal stable? She won't let me fall then,' the princess said and, reaching out, she stroked the mare's head and neck with a small hand. Sarita responded by licking her hand.

The riding lessons that began the next day soon became an obsession with the princess. Sarita had not been disobedient even once. The tenderness with which she carried the little princess on her back surprised Banamali. Time moved on. Four years passed.

During this time, Sarita had reached her full growth and Princess Sujasha too was about to step out of childhood.

Then, one fine morning, something strange happened.

Sarita, carrying Princess Sujasha on her back, trotted along the road. But that day, they had ventured beyond the outskirts of the capital. In front of them was a steep hill, studded with forbidding boulders. Sarita stopped abruptly; perhaps she wanted to turn back. But the princess wouldn't allow her to stop. She pulled at the reins and nudged the mare's belly with her feet, urging her to go on. Sarita, despite her reluctance, continued to climb, focusing her attention on the tricky slope ahead. Before she had moved a few feet, a rock slipped away from under one of her hind legs and Sarita lost her balance. Instantly, she dug her hooves into the rock and crouched low to steady herself.

Suddenly, the princess heard a voice say, very clearly, 'Princess, please dismount quickly! My feet are slipping and I might fall off the cliff!'

Since there was no one else around, it was only the mare, Sarita, that could have spoken! Princess Sujasha was astounded to hear the animal talk. 'Can you really talk in the language of humans?' she asked in surprise. 'Oh yes,' Sarita said, 'but only you can hear and understand what I say.' The young princess, her heart throbbing, managed to clamber down somehow and Sarita, with an effort, staggered back to her feet. They turned and looked down. They had climbed nearly seventy or eighty feet up the steep hill.

'Well done! You are the best mare in the world, my dear Sarita,' the princess exclaimed, stroking Sarita's neck lovingly.

'And you, my beautiful princess, are the best princess there is!' Sarita said.

After this incident, the princess and Sarita became inseparable. Sarita stood quietly at Princess Sujasha's side as she studied her book; she was there beside her when the princess received lessons in art, swordsmanship, or statecraft. Everyone was surprised, some even dismayed, by this strange attachment between the princess and a 'dumb' animal.

Then things began to happen.

One night, there was an uproar in the ladies' wing of the palace. Everyone ran into the princess's chamber to see what was happening. What they saw was amazing. The princess, instead of going to sleep, was sitting up in bed, sobbing. When asked the reason for her tears, she said that she had seen a man beating his old bullock mercilessly and driving it out of the house. The poor animal, hungry and in pain, was lying outside the palace. She demanded that the owner of the bullock should be found immediately and made to take the bullock home.

Where was this man that the princess claimed to have seen, and where was the bullock? Perhaps the princess had had a bad dream, her maids said. But the princess would not be convinced. In the end, the palace gates were opened and the king's servants went out in search of the bullock. The animal was lying outside the palace gates, just as the princess had said. After a search, its owner was traced too. Princess Sujasha went to bed only after the man had been punished and compelled to take the bullock back to his place.

Such instances grew in number as the days went by. The king and queen doted on their child and readily fulfilled all her wishes. The princess made peculiar demands: she wanted an old lion in the zoo to be set free. Men who earned their livelihood by trapping and selling birds or getting tame monkeys to perform tricks were soon out of business. So avidly did the princess pursue these whims that the royal couple did not have the heart to dissuade her. Animal slaughter was prohibited in the kingdom and people were forced to live on vegetarian food. The practice of animal sacrifice was permanently discontinued.

The day on which Princess Sujasha turned sixteen became another festival. The palace bustled with activity. Royal officials looking after different departments moved about busily, making arrangements for the celebration. Gifts in the form of money, food, and clothes were distributed among the poor. The atmosphere throbbed with excitement.

After she was through with distributing charity, the princess, clad in her divinely beautiful costume, adorned with gem-studded jewellery, rushed to the royal stables. With great affection, she fed Sarita with delicacies from the royal kitchen.

'Tell me, Sarita,' the princess asked her companion. 'How do I look in these new clothes and jewellery?'

'To me, you are always the most beautiful person on the earth, no matter what clothes you are attired in,' Sarita replied.

'My mother insisted I wear blue, although I would have preferred white. Does this colour suit me?' the princess asked.

'It suits you just fine, Princess,' Sarita said admiringly. 'I remember you dressed in blue, when you were just ten years old, darting about the garden across a carpet of lush green, looking like a butterfly from a distance. The sight is still vivid in my memory.' Here, Sarita paused, lowered her head, and made an effort to open her eyes wider. 'These days, my eyesight is getting weak and sometimes I can't tell one colour from another.'

'Why is that?' the princess asked with concern.

'That, Your Royal Highness, is what makes human beings different from us animals. By the time you reach the age when the world looks most colourful, the glamour of youth has started fading from the world of animals. Already, my eyesight and sense of smell have become feeble while your powers are at their peak. Soon I shall be too weak even to trot, let alone gallop! At my age, an animal is slaughtered if it does not die a natural death!'

'I shall never let that happen to you, Sarita!' the princess cried out.

'But that is the sad truth, my princess,' Sarita said philosophically.

The shock of the revelation was too much for the princess to bear. Her eyes filled with tears. That very day, she sent for Banamali and told him to take special care of Sarita. Banamali assured her that Sarita was receiving special care even without her asking, because the princess's attachment to her was well known.

After that day, the princess never went riding on Sarita's back, never allowed her to be taken on a long journey or run at a gallop. Instead, Sarita was moved to a peaceful grassy meadow on the outskirts of the kingdom where she was given the choicest of horse foods to eat. The princess often visited her in her retirement.

Time moved on at its own pace.

'You seem to be a little restless today,' Sarita said to Princess Sujasha when the latter was visiting her one day. Her eyesight had dimmed and she could see only a blurred image of the princess. But she rightly guessed that she was dressed in gorgeous clothes and looked ravishing.

'You know, Sarita,' the princess said, 'I met someone today while I was returning from the temple with my mother.' The princess said excitedly, 'I was waiting for the gardener to pluck some champak flowers for me, and as I hurried down the path to catch up with Mother, I suddenly found myself face to face with him.' Sujasha paused, took a deep breath, and continued, 'His name is Prince Sujay. He has just arrived in our city and is a guest in our palace. I overheard my mother tell someone that negotiations are going on for my marriage to him and he has come here to meet me.' The princess paused, fidgeted a little, and said softly, as if speaking to herself, 'He is so handsome! I'm told he is kind and gentle as well. But my father is arranging a hunting expedition for him. How could such a noble-looking person be interested in slaughtering animals? I shall ask him clearly if he will give up hunting in case we get married.' Sarita watched the princess intently. She looked excited.

'And how did Your Royal Highness find the prince? Was he up to your expectation?' Sarita asked.

'I don't know what to say,' the princess answered. 'He has a pleasing personality and he speaks in a kind voice, but who knows what lies deep inside? You can't know somebody's real nature after only a few brief meetings, can you? My parents obviously approve of the match and I guess the people of our two kingdoms would welcome the alliance. It would be to the advantage of both countries.'

'But what does your heart say?'

'Is a princess allowed to have a heart?' Sujasha said ruefully. 'She becomes the property of the state the moment she is born. Her birthday is an occasion for public celebration, and when she goes to school or learns the arts of warfare, she becomes a national spectacle—the pride of the country! Surely, a princess must be prepared to give up something in return for the honour and love the people give her.'

'Your Highness doesn't seem too happy,' Sarita said with concern. 'Is there some other suitor whom Your Highness has in mind?'

'No,' the princess cut in, 'there's nothing like that. I'm sure Prince Sujay is a fine gentleman. Still, a doubt lingers in my heart. Would a true prince hunt animals?'

The princess and Sarita kept standing in silence. After a long time, the princess trudged back to the palace.

The wedding of Princess Sujasha and Prince Sujay was a grand affair. There was great rejoicing and celebration in the country. Not just the king's subjects but even the trees in the forest shed tears as they bade farewell to the princess.

The day before the princess left for her husband's palace, she sat by Sarita's side for a long time.

'Take care of yourself, Sarita!' she advised her old friend, her voice choked with tears. 'Never stress yourself.' She stroked the mare's back fondly, heaved a deep sigh, and returned to the palace that was bustling with activity. Sujasha refused stubbornly to accept any animals—elephants, horses, or even cows, as wedding gifts.

In due course, the princess attained motherhood, giving birth to a son and a daughter. Any news of her that reached the palace was eagerly lapped up. Sarita strained her ears to pick up information about any new development in the life of her beloved princess. Despite Banamali's loving care, Sarita's health deteriorated rapidly. Her eyesight grew weaker by the day.

ॐ

'Princess Sujasha has come home. She will stay with her parents for a few days,' someone announced as he ran past the royal stables. Sarita heard the news and grew alert. She raised herself with some effort and walked slowly towards the palace garden.

Princess Sujasha saw Sarita coming from a distance and ran to meet her, after taking leave of other guests and friends. Sarita felt elated and walked faster. But as she came closer to the princess, she stopped abruptly, looking at the princess with unbelieving eyes.

Could this pale, sombre-looking figure in front of her be Princess Sujasha? Sarita looked at her closely. Yes, there still was that regal touch in her movements. But why did she look so morose? She had lost her sparkle! Sarita's heart was gripped by a morbid fear. The princess too quickened her pace as her eyes fell on Sarita. Reaching her favourite mare, Princess Sujasha held her in a loving embrace and stroked her back affectionately.

'How are you, Sarita? Did you miss me?'

Sarita could not speak. Her heart was too full.

'Is everything fine with Your Royal Highness?' she asked at last. 'How do you like your new life?'

'It is a strange country that I live in now,' Princess Sujasha said. 'They have beautiful gardens, in which they grow the most exquisite and fragrant of flowers. But no one is interested in savouring the fragrance; no one marvels at the multi-hued flowerbeds stretching for miles. Instead, the flowers are packed in cartons and exported to different countries. No one cares to look up into the night sky or gaze at the stars; nor does anyone walk barefoot through the dew-drenched grass. No one has ever known the smell of the earth after the first summer rain or listened to the river flow by on a moonlit night.'

'I understand, Princess,' Sarita cut in. 'You need not explain further.'

Both Sarita and the princess were silent for a while.

Suddenly, the princess said, 'I want to take a look at the lake at the end of the garden, where my lotus flowers used to bloom. How I have missed it!'

They walked towards the lake. Sarita followed the princess in silence.

'The lotus beds look as fresh as ever,' the princess remarked.

'It was you who got this lake dredged,' Sarita reminded the princess. 'You must have got one for your in-law's palace as well?'

'No,' the princess replied tonelessly. 'Who has time for lotus blossoms? My life has changed too! All I can do now is watch the sun go down across the western horizon. I watch the sunset day after day and wait for the next sunset.'

'And the young prince? And the little princess—why haven't they come with you?' Sarita inquired. 'We were waiting eagerly to see them.'

Sujasha was silent for a while. 'Oh, they are being well looked after there. After all, they are state treasures!'

'Let's walk to the edge of the forest as we used to do before,' she said.

Without exchanging a word, both of them walked along the path leading towards the forest on the outskirts of the kingdom.

Sujasha gazed at the stretch of forest that lay ahead, unaware of the passage of time.

At last, Sarita broke the silence. 'Your Highness, it is time for us to return. They must be looking for you in the palace. Let us go back.'

But the princess did not seem to hear her. She stood motionless, as if in a trance. In the fading glow of the departing sun, the forest appeared mysterious. It was as if the layers and layers of brooding silence, piled up over the years, had finally acquired the colour of the sunset. Flocks of chirping birds flew into the forest and disappeared into that pale red film. The atmosphere was wrapped in a strange quietude.

'I feel that my whole being has been trapped in the lingering process of decay. I must escape into this mysterious land before I am completely eliminated,' Sujasha declared, pointing at the silent forest. 'Would you like to come with me, Sarita? This is where we belong!'

Sarita did not say anything. The silence grew thicker.

Slowly, she bent her front legs and crouched low. Princess Sujasha hopped onto her back. The mare got up, with the princess on her back, and moved into the forest. There was no sign of any feebleness in her body. Both were silent as they slowly melted into the depths of the forest. The sun had almost set.

Children's Day

You can find them anywhere.

Faceless urchins in dowdy half-sleeved shirts, which might have been white at some point of time but have been soiled beyond recognition, and grimy brown knickers in similar condition; the mops of oil-less hair turned rusty, the blank look in the eyes, and the hard lines on the faces testifying to a mind that had matured before its time.

Their names could be anything—Sonu, Muna, Bhim, Chhotu, anything. Who would want to know?

You see them every day but seldom notice them. You live with them as you live with so many other creatures that apparently have no existence—the diseased stray cat, the mangy dog on the street, or the decrepit, skinny bullock that has no further use. There are so many like them, sitting on the steps of temples holding battered aluminium begging bowls or stretching out greedy hands to the window of your motor car whenever it stops. Clad in tatters, their diseased, disfigured hands and feet bandaged in dirt-smeared clothes, wind ruffling their coarse, matted hair, they always are around but never noticed.

You can't help change that.

You have to live with the truth that such pictures of poverty and decay lend our country its identity.

But Babula is different. He might once have been one among the many, but now he is indispensable to the Maa Tarini sweet shop. There could be no two opinions on that.

It is the location of the shop that gives it its advantage. Being just ten yards or so away from the bus stop on the Cuttack–Baripada highway, it was bound to draw the attention of passengers; not just the buses that plied directly from Cuttack to Baripada, but the Bhadrak-bound ones as well, stopped there for a while before taking a different route.

A faded signboard bearing the name 'Maa Tarini Sweets', held up by rusty iron wires, hangs pathetically from two rickety bamboo posts. It is precariously tilted to one side and customers carefully avoid it while entering the shop for fear it might collapse and fall on them. The harsh sun and driving rain have erased a few vowel marks, distorting the name. Beyond the signboard, there is a not-too-small, brick-walled room with a tin roof, which serves the twin purposes of kitchen and dining hall. The walls are not plastered and the room is completely open in front. A small door at the far side opens to the back of the shop. A large earthen *chula* is installed in one corner of the shop. The owner, Bata Sahu, sits by it day and night and deep-fries different kinds of mouth-watering snacks in a large pan, laying them out in large platters around the hearth. A row of cupboards with glass doors stands by the hearth, a few feet away from Bata Sahu's seat. An array of neatly arranged plates on the shelves behind the glass doors holds a tempting display of sweetmeats. Across the cupboards are some shaky tables, five in number, and a long wooden bench for customers to sit on. Years ago, the tables were painted a garish reddish brown, but are almost innocent of paint now.

Jagabandhu, a young man of twenty, takes orders from customers and waits on them. Bata Sahu treats him with deference. He always speaks to him in a mollifying voice: 'Try to be a little faster with your hands, my boy,' he tells him.

Babula's role is different; he stands at a little distance from the customers' tables, a greasy rag in his left hand, keeping a steady eye on the men eating keenly. He hastens to the table even before a customer is out of his seat, pulls away the used plate with his right hand while his left hand gives the table a quick wipe. His hands work in perfect synchronization. Jagabandhu is always on the lookout for any lapse in Babula's work. Bata Sahu, too, shouts at the boy when he is a second late in cleaning up a table. 'Hey, Babula, you idiot, why are you standing there doing nothing?' Bata Sahu snarls at him.

Babula carries the cheap steel plates and bowls out through the back door that opens onto a foot-wide veranda running along the length of the back wall. He always follows the same routine in cleaning the soiled utensils. First, he brings the leftover food close to the rim of the plate; next, scooping up the scraps in his right hand, he flings them with force into the bushes growing along the road. Every time he does that, two mangy dogs, one brown and the other black, rush in, wagging their tails, and pounce on the waste, and immediately, a nauseating stench rises from the pile of stale food that has been lying there for days. The same feeling of distaste and aversion keeps returning to Babula every time he repeats the action. There is a rusty tub filled with water at one end of the narrow veranda. The mud-coloured water never reflects Babula's face, nor has he the leisure to watch his own reflection. An aluminium mug without a handle lies at the bottom of the tub. Babula picks up the mug, water spilling from it, and holding the plate a little away from him in one hand, he splashes water on both sides of it from the mug, which he holds in the other hand. As water drips from the plate into the small ditch under the veranda, mud and dirt splatter the wall. Babula dips the plate into the tub, takes it out quickly, and hurries inside the shop as if he has suddenly remembered something important. Another customer has left the table by that time. One more is ready to leave, hastily swallowing the last fragment of puri. Babula eyes the customer's plate like a cat. The less room Bata Sahu and Jagabandhu are given to find fault with his work, the better for him, Babula thinks. He knows, however, that the reprimands come more out of habit than any desire to help him improve in his work.

Work begins early in the morning. First, puri, vada, and jalebi are fried for breakfast and potato curry prepared to go with them. Some passengers get off the early buses and have their breakfast at 'Maa Tarini Sweets'. The drivers and conductors eat to their heart's content and pay only half the normal price: this is the commission they have earned for bringing customers to the shop. Only a few regular customers, some truck and tractor drivers, and five or six autorickshaw drivers come to the shop at noon for their midday meal of coarse rice and *dalma* and fried vegetable. Vada, pakora, and samosa are fried for the afternoon customers. Sweetmeats are prepared later in the evening. It usually after midnight that the sweetmeats are stashed away in their respective containers and the shop is cleaned. Bata Sahu, Jagabandhu, and Babula eat the leftovers from the midday meal and retire for the night. Babula observes that Jagabandhu leaves the shop on most nights. 'He is going to visit some of his relatives,' Bata Sahu answers nonchalantly when Babula asks him about Jagabandhu's nocturnal escapades. As far as Babula knows, Jagabandhu has no relatives or acquaintances for miles around. But he dare not ask more.

There is another small room with unplastered brick walls and a tin roof, adjacent to the main shop. This is Bata Sahu's living-cum-bedroom. An old mattress lies on the cot that Bata Sahu sleeps on. His clothes and underwear hang from a clothesline inside the room. Rolled-up straw mats lie in a heap in one corner. The containers of sweetmeats prepared in the night are kept in another corner.

'Can I have three rupees worth of samosas?' someone asked behind Babula. There was a compelling quality about the voice that made Babula pause in his work and turn around. A pair of kind, questioning eyes was fixed on him.

'Can I have some samosas?' the boy repeated. Babula looked around to check if the request had been made to him and not to Bata Sahu or Jagabandhu. No, it was to him. It was the first time that a customer had asked him for anything and Babula felt very important. He was going to pack three samosas in a paper bag and hand it over to the boy waiting at the entrance. But how could he pick up the snacks with his dirty, unwashed hands? The boy who had asked for the samosas was a little taller than him and had a bright, dusky-brown complexion. He was neatly dressed in black shorts, held up by an expensive-looking belt, and a spotless white shirt. His feet were clad in polished black shoes and white socks. He exuded affluence. Babula stood there, undecided. The boy, in the meantime, had taken out a five-rupee note folded in two and held it out to Babula.

'Don't just stand there; give him the samosas, you idiot! Here, take this packet,' Bata Sahu shouted at him, holding the paper bag in his outstretched hand. Babula put down the plate and the bowl on a table. He took the packet from Bata Sahu and handed it to the boy who, to Babula, looked like a prince. The boy took the samosas from his hand with a smile. He suddenly pointed a finger at the sleeve of Babula's soiled and tattered shirt. There was a large tear under the right arm.

'You should ask your mother to stitch that up,' the boy said with a smile. Without a word, Babula accepted the five-rupee note which the boy handed him, took it to Bata Sahu, collected the change, and returned two rupees to the boy. The boy's fingers touched Babula's palm as he took the money. The entire exercise left Babula slightly dazed. A boy who looked like a prince had spoken to him with such courtesy and accepted snacks only from him and no one else. It was something new!

He tried to recollect the remark that the boy had made about his torn shirt. 'Ask your mother to stitch that up' or something like that. How would the boy know if Babula had a mother at all?

He remembered that he had had a mother. He had followed her around since the time he had known the world around him. She might still be somewhere. The memory of the dim figure, with a perpetually glum face and a thin body wrapped in a dirty sari, her skin singed dark brown by the sun, and wind-ruffled dry hair, came back to him. How old had she been—old or young? He couldn't say. Had she really been his mother? How could he answer that question? Perhaps he remembered her because she used to sit by the bowl of *pakhala* and the dish of under-cooked, watery potato curry, waiting for him. For the rest of the day, neither Babula nor the woman bothered about each other. They lived in a *basti* with some other men and women. He slept in one dingy room of a hut along with some other children of his age. It was as if all of them were blood brothers and sisters. In the morning, they went to the huts where their respective mothers lived, hoping they would get something to eat. Occasionally, police raided the basti. The sound of the policemen shouting abuses and the women crying could be heard in the silence of the night. The government's men, the children would be told, had pulled down their shanties and set fire to them. The next day, the group of men, women, and children moved to a different basti, carrying their scanty belongings. A new habitation was set up. Such incidents recurred every few months.

One such incident had changed Babula's life. The memory of that eventful day was still fresh in his mind. That afternoon, as he had been playing with his friends by the drain that flowed through the centre of the basti, a police jeep pulled up a few yards away. Two policewomen stormed into the hut, and the next moment, as Babula watched in fear, they dragged his mother into the open. She was trying to say something between loud sobs but Babula couldn't make out what she was saying, nor did the policewomen wait to listen. They forced her into the jeep and drove away. Babula had expected his mother to take a look back at him before she was driven away, but she didn't.

After the police jeep had left, Babula walked to the hut with heavy steps. He didn't understand what was happening, but a feeling of despair descended on him. The hut looked forlorn and desolate. For the first time, Babula looked around the hut with interest. He used to come there just two times a day to eat. He had never cared to take any notice of the things there. An old cloth mattress with innumerable patches was spread on the rough earthen floor. In one corner of the small room stood a trunk; two old saris that belonged to his mother, neatly folded, were laid over it. A hearth that looked like a small hole had been dug into the floor in another corner. Some aluminium thalis and an aluminium cooking-pot covered with a lid were kept by the hearth. As his eyes swept over these things, something turned inside his stomach. There was no mistaking the familiar pangs of hunger. What surprised him was the timing. It was an odd hour for hunger, Babula thought. But he couldn't ignore the urgency of the demand.

In a desperate effort to find some food, he ransacked the small but well-kept room. He flung the neatly placed household articles violently across the room. His mother's clothes, a couple of shabby mattresses, a small picture of Lord Jagannath, the small brass bell that his mother used to ring while she worshipped her gods, lay scattered all over the hut by the time his frantic search was over. At last, he found what he was looking for—half a bowl of stale pakhala. He gulped down the contents of the bowl, leaving out not even a grain. He felt tired after all this exercise and lay down on the floor amidst the litter. Soon he was fast asleep. It was after sunrise the next day that he woke up. He came out of the hut and looked around. There was no male member of the basti in sight. Some women were hanging clothes to dry on the clothesline outside their huts or patting cow dung into cakes, which they put out in the sun to dry. A few small children sat splashing themselves with the water that had collected in tiny puddles under the tube well. Slowly, he stepped out through the door and bolted the door from outside. He cast an indifferent glance at the hut, as though it was totally unconnected with him, turned, and walked away.

A long walk brought him to the bus stop. The milling crowd, the roar of the engines, and the smell of fried snacks filled him with wonder. The smell of food brought back the hunger. Babula soon discovered that it was not too difficult to obtain food: all that he had to do was to stretch out a hand, and some shopkeeper would put a piece of bread, a vada, or chapatti, sometimes even a *rasgola*, into it. It seemed difficult to believe he could get such delicious food with so little effort. He wondered how he could have forced himself to push stale pakhala and watery potato curry down his throat, day after day. But he also discovered that he could not depend entirely on the charity of the shopkeepers. What they fed him was rarely enough to satisfy his hunger. He began to steal from the shops. He would throw a furtive glance around to make sure no one was watching and lift a potato chop or a piece of bread from the display platter. But after a few successful attempts, he was caught red-handed. Vulgar abuse, slaps, and kicks were mercilessly showered on him. 'You will be handed over to the police if you do this again,' the men who beat him warned. 'The police will break every bone in your body!' Somehow, he managed to drag his battered body to a cement bench meant for passengers and sat down. What was he to do now, Babula thought. The future looked hopeless.

'Should you be beaten so hard just for stealing a couple of potato vadas, boy?' someone said. Babula turned in the direction from which the voice had come. An elderly man with a greying beard, wearing a soiled dhoti that came down to his knees, stood beside the bench. Babula had never seen him before. He looked up at the man, looked away the next moment, and started to sob.

'Tch, tch, how cruelly they have beaten the poor child!' the man said. 'Don't cry, my boy! But why do you have to steal? You can get enough food if you are prepared to work.'

Curious now, Babula turned to face the man.

'Will you work in a snack shop?' the man asked him. 'My nephew owns one. There is not much work to do—just mopping tables and a bit of dishwashing. You can have good food three times a day. What do you say?' Babula didn't reply. 'Come with me, I shall take you there,' the man said.

Babula wiped away his tears with the back of his hand and followed the man to the bus. They got off the bus in the late noon. About twenty feet or so away from the place where they had alighted was a snack shop, 'Maa Tarini Sweets'. The man walked into the shop, leaving Babula behind. There was another man inside the shop, of about the same age as the one who had accompanied Babula. He sat cross-legged on a wooden cot, wearing a soiled dhoti. The upper half of his body was bare. The man who had brought Babula bent down to whisper something in his ear and pointed at Babula. The man inside the shop knitted his brows and eyed Babula, giving him a quick look up and down. His lips curled in a smile. 'Come inside,' he said encouragingly, 'Why are you standing there?' Babula walked slowly towards the shop.

'What's your name, son?' the man asked. Without waiting for Babula's reply, he looked into the shop and called out loudly, 'Hey, Jaga, get some rice and curry for this boy, will you?'

The narrow room with unplastered walls that was attached to the main shop served as Bata Sahu's retiring room. Jaga pushed a worn-out straw mat towards Babula. He spread it out on the floor of the room and lay down. Bata Sahu occupied the string cot. Babula lay awake for a while listening to the loud snores of the shop-owner and the soft squeaking and pattering of rats. But the satisfaction of eating a full meal after a long time, the novelty of the place, and the luxury of the straw mat soon lulled him to sleep.

The next day too, the food was just as good. The burden of work did not seem excessive to Babula. But being new to the job, he tended to be slow. Bata Sahu, however, was not too demanding. 'You will have to work faster, boy!' he would advise Babula good-humouredly. Whenever Babula spilt a little curry while clearing the used plates and bowls, he looked at Jagabandhu with nervous eyes, but the latter only gave him a slight wink or a soft whistle, as if to say 'No problem. You will learn!' Jagabandhu's workload had been greatly reduced after Babula came and he was, therefore, quite pleased with the boy. But Babula noticed that Jagabandhu ate twice as much as he did. He left the shop as soon as it was closed for the night. Babula didn't know where he went or when he returned. Regular meals, light work, and good sleep brought about a noticeable change in Babula's appearance within a few days. The dark shadow of hunger and sorrow that had loomed over him had started to fade.

Then it happened.

It was about five days after Babula had started working at the shop.

A short shower in the evening had brought swarms of mosquitoes. Despite their incessant assault, Babula had drifted into a light sleep. Suddenly, he felt something slither over his body. Instantly, he sprang up to a sitting position.

'Shh, don't make a sound,' a hoarse voice whispered in his ear. At first, Babula couldn't recognize the voice. 'Lie still,' the man hissed through clenched teeth. Babula realized in a moment that it was Bata Sahu. Before Babula could speak, Bata Sahu had pulled down the loose knickers that Babula wore. What was Bata Sahu doing to him? Babula was astonished. The next moment, he felt a sudden stabbing pain. A howl escaped him. His whole body throbbed with that excruciating pain.

'Oh, Mother, I am dying! Please let me go!' The groans reverberated through the small room and escaped through the chinks in the door to reach the empty highway and melted away into the vast space where the agonized cries of hundreds of children are heard for a while and then disappear.

'Shut up! Calling out to your mother! That slut must be busy with god knows how many men!' Bata Sahu snarled. 'Will you keep quiet or ...,' he hissed menacingly. But Babula could not keep quiet. The pain made him whimper softly as tears of shame and agony ran down the corners of his eyes.

'Listen, you bastard! I'll slash your neck with that big knife if you don't keep quiet,' Bata Sahu muttered in disgust and sat up. He rose to his feet, unbolted the door, and moved out. A little later, Babula could hear the sound of water running from the tap and Bata Sahu clearing his throat.

The pain was worse the next morning. Babula forced himself out of the bed with tremendous effort. His legs were trembling. Bata Sahu took out a five-rupee note from the drawer of the counter where he kept the cash and offered it to the boy. Babula looked at it through eyes swollen from hours of weeping and turned his face away. Jagabandhu signalled to him with his eyes to take the note.

'Jagabandhu,' Bata Sahu said in a greasy voice, without looking at Babula, 'get a new shirt and a pair of shorts for the boy from the weekly fair, will you?' and resumed the act of frying puris.

Babula spent a restless day, and by evening, the restlessness had turned into terror. In the few days he had spent at the shop, Babula had learnt that the last bus that came along that road before the shop was closed for the night halted for only a few minutes at the bus stop, a furlong or so away. He took out the five-rupee note from the pocket and looked at it for a moment. He moved out of the back door with a look of fake urgency shadowing his face. He began to run in the direction of the bus stop as soon as he was out of the door. A few minutes later, his ears picked up the vroom of the bus and his heart began to beat fast. Suddenly, he felt a hard smack on his back and turned round to see Bata Sahu and Jagabandhu. They had followed him. Bata Sahu held an electric torch in his hand.

'You are tired of the good food and the handsome wages, aren't you?' Bata Sahu snarled at him. He struck Babula again and again. 'The next time you try to run away, I'll hand you over to the police on a charge of theft. They will lock you up in a cell forever. You will never see the outside world again.'

Bata Sahu jabbed him with the lower end of the torch. He put his hand inside Babula's shirt pocket and took away the five-rupee note after they reached the shop.

After a week or so, there was a repeat of the strange, painful act, but the intensity of the pain had receded. 'Didn't you promise to get me some new clothes?' Babula asked. The agony that he had passed through was reflected in that simple question.

'Of course, I will get it for you this week,' Bata Sahu assured him. And he kept his promise.

'Could you give me three rupees' worth of samosas?' a familiar voice said. Babula came out of the reverie and looked. It was the same good-looking boy. Babula felt he had been waiting for the boy to come back; for reasons unknown to him, he wanted to meet that well-dressed, soft-spoken boy again. This time too, the boy spoke to Babula and to no one else. Babula looked at his own hands. They were dry and clean, unlike the previous time. He ran to the counter where the platter of samosas was kept, put three in a paper bag, and handed it to the boy. This time too, the boy gave him a five-rupee note; Babula ran back to the counter to collect the change from Bata Sahu and returned quickly to the boy.

'Have one,' the boy offered before he took the two rupees.

Babula was surprised. He shook his head.

'Then keep the change. You are very poor, aren't you? Mother says one should help the poor.' Babula looked at Bata

Sahu out of the corner of his eyes and slowly lowered the hand that held the money.

'Don't you go to school?' the boy asked again. Babula did not answer this question; he just kept looking at the boy in silence. The thought of going to school had never crossed his mind.

'My name is Mohan. What's your name?'

Babula didn't answer this question either; he was feeling shy—what should he say his name was?

'Your name?' the boy insisted.

'Babula.'

'That's what they call you at home, but I am sure there must be another name.'

Silence again. Babula lowered his gaze.

'Oh, you don't have a "good name"; your parents haven't given you one. Is it because you don't go to school?'

The young man who had brought the boy on his bicycle stood waiting a little distance away. 'Muna Babu,' he called out, 'please hurry, we're getting late.'

'I am leaving now. I shall come again tomorrow. The samosa here tastes good, but my mother doesn't like my eating samosas in the bazaar. Don't tell anyone I bought samosas here.' The boy turned and walked out of the shop.

'What was the boy telling you?' Jagabandhu interrogated Babula.

'Nothing, he just wanted to know my name.'

'Oh, he seems to have taken a liking to you. Do you know who he is? The district collector's son. Why is he trying to be friendly with you?' Babula had no answer to the question. But he was suddenly filled with a new sense of elation. He carried the used dishes and glasses to the back veranda, put them down, and stood quiet for some time, savouring the feeling. He took out the two-rupee note from his pocket, looked at it, refolded it, and returned it to his pocket.

'What's your name?' he muttered softly, repeating the question that the boy had asked him. What did the boy say his name was? Yes, Mohan. What a beautiful name! He was reminded of a picture he had seen in an old calendar, of Lord Krishna holding a flute in his hands. The dark-skinned boy Krishna in the picture, smiling a beatific smile, looked enchanting. 'That is Mohan,' his mother had said. He had been looking at that calendar for longer than he could remember. Babula savoured the sound of the letters in the name and wished his own name was as lovely as that. He stood on the veranda for quite some time smiling to himself, going over the incidents of the afternoon in his own mind. A noise outside broke the spell. He washed the dishes with quick hands and came into the shop.

A small girl in a not-too-clean pink frock was crying loudly. Her carefully oiled and combed hair was done up in two short braids, each tied neatly with a length of red ribbon. Babula looked in surprise at the girl, unable to comprehend the unexpected situation. He took another step into the shop and looked closely. Two boys stood near Bata Sahu. He couldn't remember seeing them before. He moved closer to Jagabandhu and asked, 'Who are they?'

'Don't you know?' Jagabandhu whispered back, 'They are his children. There are three more of them back in his home in the village.' Babula turned to look at the children. The boys looked a little older than the girl. The three ate the evening

meal and lay down to sleep on the floor along with Babula.
Before he went to sleep, Babula heard the eldest of them
having an argument with his father.

'I have some bad news for you, Father,' the boy said, with a
note of urgency in his voice. 'Mother is too ill to get up from
bed and Kuni has been down with diarrhoea for the last four
days. Mother wants you to come home immediately.'

'How can I?' Bata Sahu snapped. 'Will you mind the shop?
How are you folks going to fill up your bellies if I sit at home?
When is your mother *not* sick—tell me! She is complaining of
one disease or another all year round. And why didn't you take
Kuni to the village *baidya*? This is the busy season for me. I
can't afford to leave the shop now. Wait till the rains come.'
Bata Sahu dismissed the topic and turned his face to the wall.

Early in the morning, the three children had puri, rasgola,
and potato curry. Bata Sahu shoved a few ten-rupee notes into
the eldest boy's hand and said, 'Don't come back here, wasting
good money on the bus fare. Write to me if you need anything.'
Bata Sahu asked Jagabandhu to look after the shop for a while
and accompanied the children to the bus stop. The little girl
didn't want to go back and cried at the top of her voice. Bata
Sahu grabbed her by the arm and practically dragged her along
the street that led to the bus stop.

'He has half a dozen kids,' Jagabandhu said in a
conspiratorial voice to Babula as soon as the four had left the
shop. 'Perhaps another is on its way—his wife is swollen like
a pitcher and can't even get up from bed. The fellow visits his
family in the village once or twice a year, starts a baby, and
then returns.' Jagabandhu wrinkled his nose in disgust and
spat into the yard in front of the shop.

The sun was going down. Babula grew more and more restless as time passed. He kept returning to the entrance of the shop, his expectant gaze rivetted to the road. And then he saw Mohan. The young man who always accompanied him was on the rider's seat and Mohan sat on the supporting rod ahead of him. They were coming towards the shop.

'He will ask for three rupees' worth of samosas, as usual,' Babula said to Bata Sahu, who too had seen the bicycle rolling towards his shop. He put three samosas into a paper bag and handed it to Babula.

Mohan saw the packet in Babula's hand and smiled. 'No samosas today,' he said. 'But I have brought these chocolates for you.' He opened his fist to show the four chocolates wrapped in shiny red, blue, green, and orange paper. Babula's eyes lit up. He stared, fascinated, at the boy's outstretched hand.

'Since you have packed the samosas for me already, I shall take them,' Mohan said. 'Satya Bhai,' he said to the man holding the bicycle, 'give him three rupees.'

'Do you know why I always buy three?' Mohan asked Babula. 'Two for me and one for Satya Bhai. But you haven't taken the chocolates, Babula. Here, have them. I brought them specially for you. Today is Children's Day and the teachers distributed chocolates among the students of our school. There were more, but I ate them up.'

'Do you know what our teacher told us today?' he went on. 'He said children are the future of the nation. They should be allowed to bloom like flowers.'

Babula kept staring at him, not knowing what to say.

'Here, take the chocolates,' Mohan said again.

Babula looked at Bata Sahu out of the corners of his eyes and held out his hand.

'I have no friends here,' Mohan said. 'They all live far away from our house. Satya Bhai plays cricket with me but there is no fun in just two people playing cricket. Have you seen my house? We can play together if you come there. Will you come?'

Babula gripped the chocolates in his hand and kept looking at Mohan, unable to speak. Just then, Jagabandhu strode past Babula to the young man called 'Satya Bhai', who sat astride the bicycle.

'What is your master's son saying to the fool?' Jagabandhu asked with a snigger.

'Do you know who he is?' he said again to Satya Bhai. 'He is Bata Sahu's whore!' Jagabandhu let out a loud guffaw and spat on the ground. A shiver of shame and revulsion ran down Babula's spine; the hand that held the chocolates trembled. His face flushed scarlet and scalding tears filled his eyes. He looked at Mohan blankly.

'What do you say? Will you come to our house and play with me? Tomorrow is a Sunday. I don't have school.' Perhaps Mohan hadn't heard Jagabandhu or understood what he had said.

Jagabandhu's mocking guffaw was heard again.

Babula kept standing like a puppet, his brimming eyes fixed on Mohan's face.

'Muna Babu, come here. Didn't Ma tell you not to mix with street children? Let's go home. We are getting late.' Satya Bhai walked up to Mohan and almost pulled him away from the shop. Mohan kept looking back at Babula, the soothing smile still hovering on his face. 'Don't you worry,' his eyes seemed to say, 'I shall come again.'

Without looking at either Jagabandhu or Bata Sahu, Babula walked out of the shop through the back door. He had no idea how long he sat on the narrow veranda at the back. Nobody asked him to come in during those long hours. Jagabandhu went away after having his dinner.

After a while, Bata Sahu came out to where he was sitting. 'Hey, boy,' he said, without looking at Babula. 'You have been sitting here all afternoon. Who is going to wash the utensils? Go, finish your work, and have some food. Jaga has laid out food for you.'

Bata Sahu washed his hands and face with water from the drum and entered his bedroom, picking his teeth. Babula heaved a deep sigh, finished washing the soiled utensils, and sat down before the plate of rice. He poured some dalma out of the bowl onto the rice, mixed the fried vegetable with it, and lifted a handful to his mouth. After he had eaten a handful or two, Babula felt that he could not eat any more. He carried the plate to the backyard and threw out its contents into the jungle of bushes by the roadside.

'Listen to me, Babula,' Bata Sahu said to him as he walked back into the shop. 'Don't pay any attention to what these people say. Aren't you living here in comfort? Who would have looked after you as I have done? If I hadn't given you shelter here, you would have starved to death or resorted to stealing. The police would have caught you and beaten you up. What will you gain by keeping company with that rich man's boy?' Bata Sahu said all this in a single breath, as if he had prepared the speech beforehand. He was a little breathless by the time he finished speaking. Perhaps he had noticed the change that had come over Babula after the evening's incident.

Babula did not reply. No sound came from him.

'Hey boy, are you there?' Bata Sahu sat up on the bed and asked. No response. He climbed off the cot and groped for Babula in the darkness. 'Why are you weeping?' he said softly as his hands felt the wetness on the boy's cheeks. 'Don't listen to that Jaga—he just talks without thinking!' Slowly, Bata Sahu's searching hands began to rove down the boy's small body as on most other nights. His breath came in short, whistling pants. Babula felt the familiar sharp, tearing pain, but made no sound. Probably, he had clenched his jaws to prevent the moans from escaping. Bata Sahu got up from the mat, wound the *gamuchha* around his waist, and unbolted the door.

A few minutes later, the silence was broken by Bata Sahu's snoring. Babula was wide awake; he stared into the darkness above. Slowly, an irregular pattern of brightness grew out of the black patch. Babula's numbed nerves jerked into life. He sat up, and as he looked, the brightness took on a shape. Babula saw a boy dressed in shining white garments. His face radiated light. Babula gaped at the figure in amazement. *Mohan*?

Yes, it *was* Mohan! How could he have come into that locked room alone at that hour of night?

Even as he watched, the luminous figure of Mohan moved through the darkness towards the door, opened it, and walked out. Babula followed him as if in a trance. Silence everywhere; even the rats and crickets were quiet. Outside, on the shelf, lay the large broad-bladed knife that was used to chop ginger and onions. Babula gripped the knife and, in one quick movement, reached the cot where Bata Sahu was sleeping. The next moment, Bata Sahu's peaceful snoring had turned into a deafening shriek of terror combined with pain, which rose to a crescendo, shattering the silence. Then the noise dissolved into the thinning darkness of the departing night.

Babula had no idea at all that he could reach the railway track by noon if he started running non-stop at the break of dawn. As he half ran and half walked along the track, a small railway station came into view almost miraculously. He drank a bellyful of water from the tap on the platform and watched the railway track that seemed to stretch up to the distant horizon. A little later, a dusty brown train, wobbly like his future, ambled into the station.

The ticket collector came to Babula who stood cringing in one corner of the compartment, looking pale and frightened. 'Ticket, ticket!' he shouted out of habit. 'Hey boy, show me your ticket. You don't have one, I suppose. God knows where these rascals come from and get into the train. No money in their pockets but they want a ride! Why didn't you buy a ticket?' Babula did not say anything. Perhaps his mind did not register what the ticket collector was saying. He just stared vacantly at him. The man moved away after examining the tickets of other passengers. Babula's hands went to his pocket, and he could feel the soothing touch of the two-rupee note that Mohan had given him. He was reluctant to part with it so easily.

'Get off the train at the next station if you don't have either a ticket or money in your pocket,' the ticket collector said to Babula threateningly, coming back to where he stood. 'And be careful not to cross my path again!'

The train began to slow down. The unknown and unseen station where Babula was to get down was probably drawing near.

The Ultimate Pay-off

Her lips curled into a smile as Ranjita remembered the lines of a folk song about a new bride that she had heard somewhere in her childhood. She was sitting on one of the steps that descended from the bank of the pond to the water. The clear still water of the pond caught her reflection. She bent down a bit and puffed softly into the water. A small ripple spread around. Her reflection in the water twirled. The image of the bride's face reflected in the mirror of water wavered out of shape. Ranjita smiled again at the thought.

It was just eight days since she had become a bride. It is customary that a bride visits her parent's home on the eighth auspicious day after marriage and Ranjita's husband had brought her here. 'Just two days,' he had told her before he left. But Ranjita had something else in her mind; she would, she thought obstinately, stay here for at least ten days. Let him miss me. Fondly remembering her husband, she reasoned with herself the next moment that it would perhaps be unjust. May be five or, in the worst case, four days; that would be fair enough.

Ranjita was not very willing to part from her husband so soon after the marriage. But it couldn't have been helped. The custom demanded it.

A cedar tree stood on the edge of the pond bending over the water. Ranjita had been watching the tree, which had stood in the same posture since her childhood. Her eyes traversed to its upper branches; an oriole perched on one of them. An oriole is believed to be an auspicious bird.

'What auspicious message are you carrying for me?' Ranjita asked the bird, raising her voice a little. The bird continued to sit there, its mind elsewhere. It just craned its neck a bit and looked at something, Ranjita could not figure out what, from the corner of its eye.

It was time to return, Ranjita reckoned. Actually, she did not want to go back so soon. She wanted to linger on sitting there alone, idly recollecting the experiences she had had in the past few days. A coy smile danced on her lips and her face blushed red as she remembered the new things that had happened to her. It was only eight days since she married, but it seemed as if an age had passed. Her world had changed.

She must leave now, Ranjita decided reluctantly. Her friends would have reached her house by now. Purnima, who had come with her eight-month-old son for a short stay with her parents, would be there. Savi and Nima too would be there, waiting for her. Mother was arranging to prepare *pitha*s stuffed with coconut scrapings for breakfast while Ranjita came to the pond to take bath.

Savi came out to greet her as soon as Ranjita reached home. 'Come, come,' she pulled Ranjita by her hand. 'Where to?' Ranjita asked. 'To the terrace. Tuna will bring the pithas here. We shall sit here and catch up.' Savi kept pulling Ranjita by her hand as they climbed the staircase leading to the terrace. Nima came next, and then Purnima, cradling her baby boy in her left arm and raising the pleats of her sari over her ankle with her right hand.

'Come on, tell us. All that happened. Don't hide anything,' Savi demanded.

'Don't feel shy. Tell us everything.' Nima, who was a comparatively reserved character, too sounded quite eager.

'Start from the beginning,' Savi persisted. 'And be frank. We want it in detail.' Flowers of innocent curiosity began to bloom in bunches on Savi's expectant face.

Ranjita swallowed.

'Why are you pestering her, you silly girls?' Purnima, who was more experienced than the others, came to Ranjita's rescue. 'Wait, you will know it all first-hand once you are married.' She turned to face Ranjita. 'I couldn't attend your marriage ceremony. That was unfortunate. Tell me about your in-laws. How many brothers-in-law and sisters-in-law do you have? And your mother-in-law and father-in law—how do you find them?

Something like an electric current ran through Ranjita's body. She was not sure whether her friends could notice her reaction. Suddenly, she remembered what had gone completely out of her mind. She remembered the stern look in her mother-in-law's eyes as she had reminded Ranjita for the third time, just when she stepped out of the door carrying the suitcase, what she must tell her parents.

'What do these girls know about marriage?' Ranjita thought gloomily. For them, marriage meant enjoying the love of the husband. They have no idea what ordeals the bride has to pass through. Well, they will know for themselves once they are married. Purnima was watching Ranjita intently. Perhaps she marked the change in her face. The coconut-stuffed pithas, along with the sweet pickle of barberry, arrived in the meanwhile. They ate and Ranjita tried to satisfy the curiosity of her friends to the best of her ability. But the words of her mother-in-law continued to echo in her mind all through. 'It was agreed upon that your father should give us one lakh cash. But he gave only fifty thousand. Wasn't it quite unfair? Why did your father have to go back upon his word? Do you know?' Her mother-in-law had asked. Though she sounded gentle, the sharp edge of the demanding note underlying the artificial softness of her voice had slashed her. 'We are decent people. That's what stopped us from cancelling the marriage. Any one in our place wouldn't have tolerated it.' She had told all this to Ranjita while she was sitting alone in her room the day after her nuptial night. Her husband was not at home, and her father-in-law was probably taking a bath. Her husband's elder sister paced about the room, pretending disinterest.

'Tell me what you know about this. Did your parents tell you anything about not paying the full amount?' Her mother-in-law repeated her question.

Ranjita shook her head and looked lamely at her mother-in-law. She was beginning to feel uncomfortable at such questions. Her sister-in-law opened her mouth. 'That won't do,' she broke in. 'The rest of the amount has to be collected by any means. It is now just six months to Mitu's marriage. Her in-laws are demanding two lakh rupees in cash from us.' Ranjita's eyes met her sister-in-law's. There was a harsh glint in her eyes that resembled the ferocious look in an animal's eyes when a prey escapes from its clutches. Ranjita cast her timid eyes down.

That very night, her husband said, 'Didn't you hear what Mother said? What your father did to us is unfair. We stomached the insult only to spare you the humiliation; because your father promised to give the rest of the amount as early as possible and begged us to go ahead with the marriage. My parents are not the people to let you get away with this so easily. Keep that in mind.'

The warning note was loud and clear.

Ranjita kept in mind what her husband had said. But there was nothing she could do about it.

Her mother-in-law broached the topic once more the next day. This time, her husband and her father-in-law were there with her. 'You have to bring the remaining fifty thousand by any means when you return.' Her voice held a note of finality. 'No one must take undue advantage of our civility in this manner.'

Ranjita did not say a word. There was nothing to say.

'Come back in two days,' her husband had said while leaving here. 'And don't forget what Mother has said,' he had added with a smile.

How could such an important thing go completely out of her mind? Ranjita was angry with herself. The *pakhala* her mother had so lovingly dished out for her, the tasty pickle stored in earthen pots, the intimate quietude at the bank of the village pond, and the fond curiosity of her childhood friends had temporarily blotted out the bitter urgency.

Evening came.

Ranjita stood alone on the terrace, her heart caught in the vortex of a terrible dilemma. A bright moon had come up in the sky some time ago and cast a silver glow all around. The

silvery light filtered through the wattles of the coconut trees
and made irregular luminous patches on the terrace. Ranjita
stood still, her face and body partially lit up by the moon. She
could have stood there for hours basking in the moonlight had
it been some other day. She climbed down the stairs, dragging
one heavy step after the other.

She found her mother busy cutting vegetables for the curry
that was to be served for dinner. 'Let me do it,' Ranjita offered,
sitting by the vegetable cutter. 'No, no,' her mother stopped her;
'you are here only for a couple of days. You needn't do all this.'

'Is Father not home yet?' Ranju asked, her eyes travelling
around. 'What is it that keeps him out till so late?'

'He must have gone to that Sarat Sahu. That swindler had
bought our fertile land at a throwaway price. He said he would
pay one lakh for it, though the market price of that land must
not have been less than at least a lakh and a half. The crop that
land yielded used to sustain us through the year. And just see
the villainy of the man—he has not yet paid the total amount
though he has got the papers of the property transferred in his
name. He has given only half the amount and had promised
to arrange the rest fifty thousand within a period of ten days.
Every day, your father goes to his house and waits till late
evening to meet him. But the man keeps on eluding him.'
Ranjita's mother breathed out a deep sigh.

Ranjita shrank inwardly. She was the reason behind the
humiliation her father was passing through, she thought
bitterly. It is she who has deprived the family of its fruitful
land and compelled them to buy foodgrains from the market
throughout the year. 'What are you all going to do now? You
have to depend on the market for everything,' Ranjita intoned.

'That's not a big problem and don't you burden your head with that. So many people are buying their foodgrains from the market. What is so unusual about it?' her mother said evasively. 'Go and get the black gram cleaned and washed. I have to put the curry on the stove for cooking.'

Something seemed to prick at Ranjita's heart.

Her brother's wife had worn a sulky look since morning. She did not speak either to Ranjita or her mother properly. 'Daughters here always have a lion's share; no one cares for the sons,' she grumbled grudgingly. Ranjita's brother could have got the job if the fifty thousand rupees spent on her dowry had been given as a bribe. The reality hit her with full force as she pondered over the remarks of her sister-in-law more seriously. Her brother was badly in need of that job. He had his wife and a two-year-old son to support. Their father had a small job in a fertilizer company. It was tough on him to run a big family with the meagre salary he was paid. He had another daughter who was to be married off in a year or two, and a son whose studies needed to be taken care of. And his retirement was due in a few years. What would happen after that? The overwhelming realization swept away the aroma of the coconut-stuffed pancakes and the delicious homemade pickle from Ranjita's memory and brought her face to face with a future that stared bleakly at her. She sat quietly on the veranda, resting her cheek on her palm, her mind caught in turmoil.

Someone switched on a torch and the light fell on her face. 'Why, isn't it our Ranjita? Why are you sitting here alone?' A familiar voice inquired from the darkness.

Father!

Ranjita was startled out of her thoughts. 'Oh, no! Was just relaxing,' she said conciliatorily. 'But why are you so late, Baba?'

Her father did not reply. He let out a sigh and walked to the well in the courtyard to wash his feet.

Power failure was a regular thing in the suburban area where they lived. There was no power since the evening. Even in the dim light of the kerosene lamp, Ranjita could notice the shadow of gloom that hung over her father's face as she ate her night meal sitting with her father and brother. Her sister-in-law ladled out the food, her face clouded, and asked if Ranjita would want a second helping of rice, her voice distant and cold. Her brother, looking glum, silently nibbled at his food. Mother fanned them with a hand fan.

'Haven't you cooked fish?' Father asked abruptly, as if remembering something.

'It is Thursday today,' Mother reminded him.

'Oh!'

'What did Sarat Sahu say today? Did he give you the rest of the money?' Ranjita's brother asked expectantly, raising his eyes from the plate but without looking straight at his father. Ranjita noticed that her brother had hardly eaten anything.

'No. He made the same old excuse. He had no money with him at present, but he would pay in a couple of days,' Father replied dryly. Ranjita was shocked at the grim despair in her father's voice. She couldn't believe that the voice of her father, who always looked at life positively, could sound so desperate.

'I will murder that scoundrel,' her brother snarled. 'Would my job keep waiting for his "a couple of days"?' The muscles in his face looked tight and swollen in the patchy light of the lantern.

'Wait, finish your food,' Mother called after him anxiously as he rose and walked away from the kitchen without eating. 'Let us wait for two days and see what happens.' There was more helplessness than conviction in her voice.

Ranjita could realize that something beyond their control had taken her family in its lethal grip. Disturbing thoughts that moved around her own marriage, her elder brother's elusive job, and the look of innocence on the sleeping, pale faces of her younger brother and sister kept her awake late into the night.

Her husband was not at home when Ranjita arrived at her in-law's house. Father-in-law, too, was out somewhere. Her mother-in-law came out in quick steps and looked at her face for a brief moment. A shiver of a fear that Ranjita could not define shook her all over. Without uttering a word, her mother-in-law stomped out of the drawing room. Ranjita's brother put down her suitcase on the floor and prepared to leave. 'Wait a little,' Ranjita said, 'I shall get you a cup of tea.'

'Give me only a glass of water. I am getting late.'

He pushed the water down his throat in quick gulps and hurried out. Almost immediately, her mother-in-law entered. 'What happened?' she demanded.

Ranjita looked at her innocently, saying nothing.

'I'm asking you,' she said sharply. 'What happened? Did you bring it?'

'The man who has to pay the money, the one who bought our land, is making the delay, Maa.' The words spurted out of her mouth although it was not in her nature to lie. 'Father has promised to come here with the money as soon as the man pays.'

'I knew it,' the older woman retorted with vehemence. 'These people would make several such false excuses for not making the payment in time once they achieved the end. I had warned both the father and son to have the money under our hold before going ahead with the marriage. Neither of them listened to me. God knows what charm the old man had cast over them. Okay, let Bana come today ...' her mother-in-law said loudly, aiming at no one in particular. The harsh glitter in her eyes and the threat in her voice chilled Ranjita's blood.

Ranjita had no idea what her mother-in-law told her husband, but he wore a sullen and grim look all through the evening. She decided to explain everything to him in the night. But her husband, without speaking a word to her, lay down on the bed turning his face to the other side. The humiliation of being dismissed so rudely hurt her deeply. A few drops of tears rolled down her cheeks and wet the pillow.

If Ranjita had hoped to find a change in her husband's behaviour the next morning, she had to encounter disappointment.

The morning after, while getting dressed for office, Ranjita's husband shouted at her. 'There is not a single shirt that is ironed. You have come back since last afternoon. What have you been doing all the time?' he demanded without looking her in the face.

'Sorry, I hadn't noticed. I shall iron them in the noontime.'

'Noontime?' he shot back. 'What the hell am I going to wear to office just now?' he yelled. As her eyes that had already widened at this unexpected reaction grew wider, a slap hit her hard across the face. She stood rooted, her face drooped lower.

Her husband left without having breakfast. Her younger sister-in-law had already left for college. Her husband's elder sister, who had come to attend the marriage, in the meanwhile had returned to her home. Ranjita's mother-in-law pointed at the clothes piled up on the cement platform of the well and the used utensils that lay in a heap nearby, gesturing to her to clean them, and went inside the kitchen.

'Come on, call your father and talk to him.'

That evening, in the presence of all the family members, her mother-in-law ordered her.

'We don't have a phone in our house,' Ranjita said slowly.

'I know that,' her mother-in-law retorted stubbornly. 'Call your neighbour's house and ask them to call your father and ask him to get the money by tomorrow by any means.'

Meekly, Ranjita obeyed her orders. After five minutes or so, her brother came on the line. The news her brother gave her had the reasons for making her both happy and morose at the same time. Her brother had, finally, been assured of the job. That made Ranju relieved. The latter half of the news, however, was not so relieving. Since money was given away as bribe for her brother's job, it was not possible for her father to arrange the amount immediately as her mother-in-law desired. But her brother promised that at the earliest, from his salary, he would pay back.

'Well, what did he say?' the questioning eyes of her mother-in-law were fixed on her face.

'A bribe of fifty thousand rupees had to be paid urgently for procuring my brother's job,' Ranjita answered meekly. 'But Brother has promised to pay the money from his salary maximum within six months. Father has requested you to wait for a few months,' she said imploringly, her voice heavy.

'I see—did you say six months? Did you hear that, Bana,' her mother-in-law turned to speak to Ranju's husband. 'These people do not intend to give us the rest of the money. Okay, they will be taught a lesson,' she declared. There was a note of foreboding in her voice. It was as if a bombshell was dropped. Everyone was too shocked to speak. Complete silence hung in the air for a few moments. Slowly, very slowly, her head drooping, Ranjita stepped out of the room and entered the kitchen.

☙

'Don't you worry, Brother has promised to pay the amount in six months at any cost,' Ranjita said solicitously, looking at her husband, who lay on the bed, gazing at the ceiling, puffing at the cigarette. Then her eyes opened wide. 'Have you been drinking?' she asked in surprise.

'So what?' he snapped. 'Have I been drinking with your father's money? So, your father needs six months to pay, isn't it?' her husband said with a sneer. 'The daughter seems to be smarter than the old man.'

Ranjita was yet to come out of the shock. She looked at her husband with unbelieving eyes.

The bedroom light was on. Her husband lay on the bed, the cigarette glowing between his fingers.

'What the hell are you gaping at me for?'

Ranjita stood speechless, stunned at the brazen audacity of the statement.

'Hmm—now start marching. Left, right, left ...' he commanded.

Ranjita stood there, stunned and miserable, trying to decide if she had heard him correctly.

'Are you going to march or shall I get up?' he snarled.

She walked a few steps, afraid that her husband would do something unexpected unless she obeyed.

'Do it correctly—left, right, left,' he shouted, his voice slurring under the impact of the alcohol. 'Come on, quick.'

Ranjita stood still, her eyes brimming. She raised her right hand to wipe away the tears running down her cheeks or may be to hide her face.

'This won't do.' He jumped off the bed and stood in front of her. The next moment, Ranjita felt something burning into the flesh just above her left elbow. A scream of agony escaped her.

'Stop howling, you fool—keep your mouth shut.' Her husband hissed and, once again, pressed the burning end of the cigarette to her elbow. This time, he held it pressed to her flesh for quite some time. Terror forbade Ranjita to open her mouth. Her husband turned off the light, and using both his hands, he flung Ranjita across the bed like someone dumping a heap of garbage in the dustbin. The excruciating pain of the experience that followed the act numbed her senses. It was as though a flock of bloodhounds mauled her body. She felt that something very delicate, stored with utmost care under several layers of consciousness deep inside her, was ruthlessly mutilated by savage jaws and claws. Her very being was mangled by some brutal, marauding force.

Her days fell into a pattern thereafter, ugly but regular. They began with torture and ended with pain. Almost every day, in different hours, she received a generous amount of different forms of beating from her husband, his mother, and his sister. Someone would bang her head onto a wall or a pillar; another would spin her a round or two, holding her by her hair. To receive kicks and slaps had become a routine matter. Ranjita had somehow managed to adapt herself to the humiliation and pain. She clung desperately to the hope that her agony would be over when, at the end of six months, her brother would pay the rest of the dowry to her in-laws.

In the meanwhile, she had been forced a number of times by her in-laws to call her father to remind him about the money. But she was strictly forbidden to write letters to her parents. Ranjita obeyed all instructions; she had no alternative. Her father had visited her a couple of times. He looked pale and drawn, and somehow frightened. The soul-consuming indifference with which he was received at his daughter's house compelled him to leave the place as soon as possible. Even waiting to gulp down the cup of tea which Ranjita brought him needed an effort.

Time moved on.

And quite unexpectedly, something happened that took everyone by surprise. Ranju developed nausea and occasional vomiting; her head reeled, and a strange sloth overtook her. 'She is with child,' Aunt Manu, the next door neighbour, remarked. The revelation was shocking. Pregnant! How could be that possible? How could a delicate human life be created in all those bone-wracking moments of animal fornication? It was her baby, and her husband's—Ranjita thought bitterly. It was a baby that found its way to her womb through hatred, fear, and abominable cruelty. The beatings and abuses she received constantly from her husband and his family members had never allowed her time to nurture the fond dream of motherhood. Despite all that, the baby was made and had started growing in her womb.

And finally, the six months were over.

After six months, a desperate phone call from Ranjita compelled her father to come to her in-laws' house. He looked even older. He sat wordlessly, his head hung low, and swallowed all insults and abuses hurled at him. Her mother-in-law announced the final decision. Ranjita's father must take his daughter back to his house and bear all the responsibilities of the mother and the child. He would never try to contact her in-laws in future and would forget all about the marriage.

'Please, don't,' Ranjita's father clasped the hands of her father-in-law and begged. 'My son is still without a job; the interview was cancelled, but it will be held in the coming two or three months. He will bring you the rest of the money immediately after he gets the job,' he promised. He had arranged ten thousand, Ranjita wondered how, and prayed her mother-in-law and father-in-law to accept that. They took the money after a lot of entreaties as if they obliged her father by accepting it.

Her father left. But before leaving, he made several appeals to her parents-in-law, ignoring all the humiliation he suffered at their hands. But Ranjita's husband and his parents had concluded that they had been outrageously cheated.

Things worsened the next day when her husband, returning from office, brought the news that his sister Mitu's would-be in-laws demanded one lakh rupees in advance. They would not go ahead with the engagement unless their demand was met. It was not possible to arrange as big an amount in such a short notice. It was obvious that Mitu's engagement would be cancelled. The despair and the humiliation it caused was unbearable. And the bitter rage born of the experience made her husband, his sister Mitu, and their parents almost insane. Ranjita's heart bled for her family, which, despite all the pain and suffering she went through, she had accepted as her own. But she couldn't think of a way to help them out of the impasse. Her mother-in-law had already taken away whatever little jewellery she had brought at the time of her marriage. She had nothing else with her to help them with.

Her husband and her mother-in-law talked for a long time.

Ranjita had no idea what all they talked about. She sat on the veranda knitting tiny socks for her unborn baby with the yellow wool her brother's wife had sent.

'Come to the kitchen,' her husband said, coming out of her mother-in-law's room.

Ranjita looked up at him demurely. There was a strange restlessness about him and his face glowed with a savage determination.

'Get up,' he ordered. Ranjita could not decide what exactly he wanted.

'Get up, I say. Quick.' He gripped her right arm and pulled her to her feet. The tiny socks, still held by the knitting needle, fell from her lap. The bundle of yellow wool dropped too and rolled down to the courtyard below the veranda. Ranju stood there, her eyes following the rolling bundle of wool.

'Come to the kitchen,' her husband hissed through his teeth.

'Mitu,' he called out to his sister. 'Bolt the front door and keep guard. Don't let anyone in,' he instructed her. Ranjita's father-in-law was not at home. Her mother-in-law stood at the door of the kitchen.

'Come on, move,' her husband ordered once again and dragged her along the veranda to the door of the kitchen. Her mother-in-law, who stood waiting there, shoved Ranjita inside. Her husband followed her into the kitchen. Ranju turned to look at the wool bundle lying in the courtyard. The half-knit socks must have fallen there too. It was muddy under the veranda, Ranju thought ruefully. The socks must have got mud on it. She felt an urge to rush out and pick up the socks and the wool bundle from the mud. But her mother-in-law stood blocking the door.

Ranjita stopped to look at her husband. His face held a brutal ferociousness that stung her heart like shrapnel. He pushed Ranjita forward. Caught off balance, she fell on the stove. Her mother-in-law handed him a bottle containing some kind of liquid. Her husband removed the cap and poured the liquid on Ranjita, soaking her all over. He appeared as cool as if he was soaking a shirt. The next moment, the strong smell of kerosene filled the kitchen room. But Ranjita did not utter a word of protest. She knew that she did not stand a chance with them; she hadn't had the power even to pick up the half-knit socks from the courtyard....

Her husband took out a few matchsticks and lit them one by one. Ranjita noticed that his steady, firm fingers made the stick catch fire with a single scratching. He threw the burning sticks on the stove. As soon as the flames rose, her husband and his mother went out of the kitchen, leaving Ranjita and the burning stove inside.

The bride that had kept quiet all this time now began to scream frantically. It was no longer the burning agony of humiliation or emotional suffering. It was real fire that had started to lick at her defenceless body. As the red and yellow flames began to leap wildly across the kitchen, Ranjita's husband, her mother-in-law, and sister-in-law started shouting for help. The dancing flames and the ear-splitting howls transformed the kitchen into an exploding inferno.

Amidst the commotion, someone had stealthily slid back the bolt and opened the front door. The screams for help calling in the witnesses and spectators began to trail outside through it.

A Shadow in the Mirror

The sacred flames leapt high as the priest poured ghee into the *havan kund* on the altar. It was the night of my wedding. Lata, my bride, sat beside me. The priest put Lata's right hand on my upturned right palm and joined our hands with a length of sacred *kusha* amid the chanting of mantras.

I raised my eyes and saw *him*!

He stood just in front of me, his eyes rivetted on the marriage altar.

A shudder passed through me. I closed my eyes but I was not able to resist the urge to have another look.

He stood there in the same posture, his eyes fixed on me, handsome as a prince in a glamorous outfit, looking exactly as he might have looked in the costume of Arjuna, had he played the role twenty years ago....

Was I hallucinating?

I looked at my watch. It was close to three in the morning. All the guests, invitees, and relatives had gone back; only the elderly members of both families and a few very close relations were present.

I dared not look up. But the urge was too overpowering to be ignored. My eyes fell on him once again and I was once again caught in the crossfire of reality and illusion. Why should he appear before me now, on this festive occasion? He had not shown himself, not even once, in these twenty years. Why tonight then?

I looked again, but he was nowhere in sight. I breathed out a deep sigh.

Lack of sleep and the fast that I had had to keep all day as the bridegroom were beginning to tell on me. I felt exhausted. Could my eyes be playing tricks?

Must be the stress, I decided.

There was a brief interval before the final rituals were performed. Lata and I got to our feet.

I stole a glance at my father, wondering if he too had noticed him. But his face registered no emotion. He seemed to be happily discussing things with my uncles. There was some time remaining for the last rituals. I tried to relax in the room intended for the bridegroom. But there was no respite from the teasing by Lata's cousins. 'Why does our brother-in-law look so faded—has the heat from the sacred flame tired him out?' someone remarked in jest. 'Why should he look faded?' another voice chimed in, laughing. 'Hasn't he married our fresh-as-a-flower sister, Lata?' There was a chorus of mischievous giggles. I desperately wanted to be alone. I wished everybody would be quiet for at least a while. But they kept on badgering me until I was called back to the altar for the rest of the rituals. Once again, I glanced at my father but failed to notice any sign of worry on his face.

The wedding ceremony was over.

We were back in my three-roomed government quarters. Certain post-wedding rituals had to be performed in the bridegroom's home. Lata's father wanted the ceremonies on the *chouthi* to be celebrated at my residence in town. Although my house was not spacious enough to accommodate the relatives and guests, my father had agreed. It was decided that Lata and I, along with the rest of the family, would leave for our village after the *saptamangala*.

My mother was busy arranging the furniture and other gift articles that had been sent along with the bride. She was giving instructions to the other ladies on how the sweetmeats and other items of food were to be distributed among neighbours and relatives. Her face revealed no sign of any disturbance; like Father, she was totally preoccupied. Even normally, she is hard-working and exceptionally active; I cannot remember seeing her resting at any time. She had been the daughter-in-law in a large joint family. Besides, she was so good at organizing such family events that her services were always in demand by relations and neighbours. She was busy now in advising, ordering, directing, and requesting people whom she had entrusted with different responsibilities.

So, Mother had not seen him either, I guessed. It must be just my imagination. It could be some relative of Lata's. But why should there be such a striking resemblance? Or had I imagined the resemblance? But why should I confuse him with someone else? And after such a long time? Wasn't it absurd? Was it because his unconscious memory had haunted me through all these years even though my conscious mind had rejected it? I found no convincing answer.

Why me then? Was it because I lacked the courage to think beyond it?

That night, Lata and I talked about a variety of subjects, mostly in a lighter vein. The wedding night, I had been told, is a night of dreams and romance for every young couple. Lata must have nurtured many such dreams in her heart. And perhaps my response was not up to her expectations.

'Why do you look so pale?' she asked. 'You seem to be stressed out since the day of the wedding. Are you all right?' I liked the easy manner in which she assumed her new responsibilities as a wife.

I could no longer hold back the question that had kept haunting me.

'Is there a young boy in your family, a boy of about fifteen or sixteen?'

Lata looked at me in surprise. Obviously, she had not expected such a question on this night—a night that she should have expected to cherish, like all other newly married girls. She wouldn't understand the agony I was passing through. 'Yes,' she said, without much warmth, 'there may be some—relatives perhaps. But why do you ask?'

'Could I have their names and address?' I asked eagerly, ignoring her question.

There was a thoughtful pause. Then she looked straight into my eyes. 'Yes, of course. I can get their address when I go home. But why do you need this information so urgently?' Her eyes held a look that was a blend of astonishment and accusation. 'What an absurd question for a husband to ask his bride on their wedding night!' the look seemed to say. I remained quiet for a moment.

'Because I saw a boy in your house who looked exactly like Bhai, my elder brother who died twenty years ago!' I said.

She stared at me in disbelief. Her lovely eyebrows arched a little, but the next moment, the lines of astonishment on her forehead dissolved. Her face softened. 'How is that possible? It must be your imagination. On such auspicious occasions, we usually remember the people we have loved. I have heard of the mishap, but ...' She stopped abruptly.

'Bhai was six years older than me. He was fifteen when he died and I was nine. It happened twenty years ago.' I could not go on. Lata moved closer to me. She held my right palm lightly between hers.

'He would have been thirty-five now, had he lived, isn't that right?' Lata asked softly.

I could no longer hold back the sob that was rising inside me like a raging storm. I broke into tears. Lata held my head between her palms and gently drew it closer. I wept like a child. 'Please calm down,' she said soothingly, as she ran her fingers tenderly through my hair. 'Don't you know that a man's lifespan is decided by fate? These things are preordained. He lived as long as he was destined to live.'

The rituals of the saptamangala were performed in my home. We left for our village the next day. My father had planned to host a feast for the people of the village on the following day. In the evening, I took Lata with me to the mango grove at the end of the village. I showed her the spot where Bhai's lifeless body had lain twenty years ago. The mango tree from which he had fallen was no longer there. My father had got it felled a few days after the tragedy.

A few days later, we went to Lata's parents' home. Lata sat surrounded by her cousins and friends, busy satisfying their curiosities about her experiences at her in-laws.

'My experiences on the nuptial night!' I overheard Lata say, her voice touched with a mild note of sarcasm. 'I have heard of husbands saying so many romantic things to their wives on that occasion. But your brother-in-law—' She stopped abruptly as she caught sight of me.

֎

Strange though it may seem, Niru had few friends of his age, and those few he did not consider important. His interest was focused on boys of an older age, friends of his elder brother. Niru knew Bhai's friends did not want a younger boy like him to be hanging around them, especially when they talked about girls. But Niru followed at his brother's heels, feigning ignorance. The older boys could not openly ask Niru to go away for fear of offending his elder brother. As an alternative, they used him to run errands for them. If at one time it was, 'Hey, Niru, go home and get some salt and green chillies', at some other time, it would be, 'Niru, go to Bula bhai's house and get the kite and the spool of thread kept in the attic.' As Niru turned to leave, Bhai would call out, 'Be careful, Niru, don't touch the processed thread. It has been coated with powdered glass and will cut your fingers!' Bhai was always concerned about Niru's safety.

Unlike his brother, Niru was very good at maths. Things like addition subtraction, and multiplication confused Bhai and arithmetical problems were like brain-wracking riddles. He used to confess his weakness at times when he was alone with Niru. 'Just help me solve this problem, Niru: a tub has two taps. Water enters the tub through one and flows out through the other. They ask you to work out how long it would take to fill up the tub with water when both taps are open. You explain it to me!' Bhai would ask in all seriousness. 'Why does our maths teacher give us such absurd problems to solve?'

But when it came to English literature, no one could match Bhai. He seemed to have an ingrained passion for the subject. Niru never liked literature. It was so tedious! And, the strangest subject of all was history! Bhai loved acting on the stage. He performed in school plays and plays organized by the club in their village. Father wanted to make his elder son an engineer. He had never approved of Bhai's interest in drama. 'Worthless boy!' he would reprimand Bhai. 'You will end up as a daily labourer and dig ditches to earn your livelihood.' He didn't mind the expenses on Bhai's education. Niru had once overheard his father telling his mother that he would sell a patch of farmland if necessary, to educate Bhai. Bhai used to laugh away the seriousness with which Niru reported such things to him.

'Father has no idea of what I have planned for my future,' Bhai said when they were alone. 'I will write plays—I will be a great playwright. I will travel around the globe staging my plays. You will see! The whole world will honour me one day,' Bhai would say dreamily.

Father detested Bhai's interest in acting in plays. He sometimes called Bhai a *maichia* when he was angry with him. Bhai's handsome face flushed crimson. Niru did not understand why his father was so hostile.

Bhai was Niru's role model—the strongest, bravest, and most clever person on this earth. He felt dwarfed by Bhai's overpowering personality. Niru was much shorter than most boys of his age. He wished he was tall and slim, like his brother, with his supple body, thick mop of hair, and a thin moustache! He hated his own shabby looks.

Bhai was the unchallenged leader of the boys of the village. No one dared touch Niru for fear of incurring his brother's displeasure. When he got angry, Niru would fight with his friends, but they fought back. Only Niru was allowed to attend the feast at which Bhai and his friends cooked: no one else's younger brother enjoyed this privilege.

Summer arrived, and so did the summer holidays.

An opera called *Draupadi's Swayamvar* was to be staged on the open-air stage in the village and preparations were in full swing. The long opera would be staged, in two parts, on successive nights. Only eight days were left for the stage performance.

Bhai and his friends were busy from morning to evening in rehearsing the play. Sania bhai would play the role of Draupadi while Bhai played Arjuna. The greater part of Niru's day was spent watching the rehearsal. He was fascinated by the way Bhai performed the role and his flawless dialogue delivery.

That day ...

Niru spent the morning at the clubhouse watching the rehearsal. He came home and ate his midday meal of pakhala and fried fish. 'Don't you go to that clubhouse in this scorching heat,' his mother had warned him. 'Here, lie down by my side and sleep.' Mother moved a little to make room for Niru on the rush mat she lay on. But sleep eluded him. He lay by his mother, awake, waiting for her to close her eyes. Father was lying on a wet *gamuchha* that he had spread out on the outer veranda, to counter the heat. Careful not to make any sound, Niru sat up and peered at his mother. She was asleep. Slowly,

Niru put aside the end of Mother's sari that covered him partially and came out of the room. A cat was prowling about the kitchen. Niru drove the cat away and went inside the kitchen. There was some pakhala in an earthenware cooking pot. Beside it, on a bell-metal plate filled with water to its rim, was a bowl. A *peedha*, upturned, had been kept on top the bowl as a lid. Niru lifted the peedha and looked. There were two big pieces of fried fish inside the bowl. Bhai hadn't eaten his midday meal. Mother had, therefore, kept his food protected from ants by keeping the bowl in a plate filled with water. The peedha was placed over the bowl to keep it out of the cat's reach. Niru replaced the peedha on top of the bowl, bolted the kitchen door from the outside, and tiptoed out of the door into the backyard. Once out of the house, he half ran and half hopped to the venue of the rehearsal.

Bhai stood holding in his hands a bow made of bamboo, with the bowstring pulled taut, ready to release the arrow. The games teacher of their school, who was directing the play, held the script. He was prompting and Bhai repeated the lines. Sania bhai, who played Draupadi, stood a little distance away, carrying a rope in both hands, as though holding a garland of flowers. Like Bhai, he, too, wore a pair of knickers. The boys who were playing other roles in the opera stood around them. Bhai was reciting his monologue, lifting the bow above his head, his eyes fixed on the floor. Niru squeezed his way through the crowd of spectators to get a closer look at the scene.

'No, no, that was not right. Do it again,' the director of the play said. He came up to Bhai and straightened his hands a little. Niru tried to get a better view. Bhai released the arrow aiming at a point above. Sania bhai walked up to him and slid the rope garland around his neck. The crowd clapped. Bhai's role was over. He wiped the sweat off his face with the ochre-coloured napkin he had wound around his waist and walked out of the crowd to the side of the stage where Niru stood. 'Bhai,' Niru said, trying to draw his attention. 'What is it?' Bhai asked.

'Father wants you at home immediately. You haven't had your midday meal. Come and eat.'

'Wait a moment,' Bhai said absent-mindedly, watching intently the performance of the other actors.

'Hey, Bhai,' Niru warned, 'Father is waiting for you with a cane in his hand. He is very angry. Come at once!'

Bhai let out a sigh. As his role was over, he said, 'Okay, let's go.' Niru followed him.

Bhai kept on reciting his lines loudly as they passed through the mango orchard.

Behold
My arrow will tear this fish
Into a hundred pieces!
How long can your lies prevail?
How long can a water-mark last
On the forehead?
Can darkness conquer the sun?

I will slash this fish of gold,
In no time it'll come hurtling down
And sprawl on the floor.
Behold, oh behold!

He carried on with his recital, his mind full of the opera. 'You will see, Niru—one day I shall write better plays than this. Spell-binding plays!'

'Hey Bhai, look,' Niru called.

'What's it?' Bhai stopped and looked back.

'Look at the mangoes hanging from the branches of that tree. Aren't they big?' Niru pointed at the mangoes. 'There's no one around. Let's pluck some,' he suggested.

Bhai looked up, following Niru's gaze.

'You are right. They have grown to full size. What do you say—shall we pluck them now?' Bhai looked at Niru. 'All right, you keep watch. Let me know if someone comes this way. I'll get a few of them and come down in a second,' Bhai said and climbed up the tree effortlessly. Niru knew that he was an expert tree-climber, but the tree was exceptionally tall and dense. Niru couldn't see the top of the tree though he bent his head backwards as far as it would go. He could not see Bhai clearly; nor did he have any idea of how many mangoes he had plucked. But the enchanting aroma of ripening mangoes filled his nostrils.

Niru remembered the day when Bhai had climbed the palm tree. The palm trees along the edge of the pond were laden with ripe, heavy fruits. Their ripe fruits fell off the trees into the slime on the bank and got spoilt. It was decided that the ripe palms should be plucked before they fell off. Bhai climbed up the tree. He plucked the palms and collected them in his ochre-coloured gamuchha. His friends and some other village boys stood on the bank watching him. Niru was there too. Suddenly, one of the boys saw a grey-brown snake climbing up the tree and let out a scream. Bhai had an ingrained fear of snakes. 'Don't you step down into the pond,' he used to frighten Niru, 'there are snakes in the water!' Bhai cast one quick glance at the climbing reptile and took a dive into the pond. All the ripe palms he had collected went into the water. Bhai swam back to the bank, empty-handed. 'That snake was not poisonous,' he said, trying to sound casual, but Niru knew he was scared of snakes. The memory of the incident tickled Niru. Once again, he looked up at the mango tree. He could see Bhai now. He had climbed to quite a height and stood precariously poised on a slender branch that bent under his weight. His gamuchha looked swollen. He must have collected a lot of mangoes, Niru thought happily.

Niru took another glance at the tree and saw just a little of Bhai. A mischievous smile crossed his face.

'Hey, Bhai, look at that yellow snake climbing the tree,' Niru shouted. 'My god, it's a cobra! It has reached a branch close to you,' he screamed and smiled.

'Oh God, where?' Bhai's startled, panic-stricken voice came from the tree. The next instant, there was a loud thud that sounded like an explosion. Niru shut his eyes tight in terror. After a moment that seemed like an age, he slowly opened his eyes and looked.

Bhai lay flat on the ground, face up, his right leg twisted at an awkward angle. Niru ran up to him. There was a glazed look in Bhai's open eyes that stared up into the mango tree. The upper row of teeth was visible through his open mouth. His ochre-coloured gamuchha lay at a little distance from him. A few mangoes rolled out of it.

'Bhai!' Niru called in a choked voice. There was no reply. Bhai looked like a stranger. Niru stared at him, hypnotized. A dark-brown liquid began to flow out in a thin line from the rock that his head lay on. Slowly, it spread on the ground and formed a tiny pool. Niru stood rooted, a blank look in his eyes.

People ran towards the mango orchard calling out to one another. Some of them lifted Bhai. The back of his brown knickers was soaked in red. His head hung down. A tuft of curly hair stuck to the sweat on his forehead.

'Blood!' someone screamed.

Within seconds, a large crowd had gathered, like the crowd that gathers to watch an opera.

Niru raised his head and saw his father running from the other end of the orchard towards the spot where they stood. There was a look of terror in his eyes. His feet slowed as he neared the spot. He appeared to be dragging one foot after another laboriously, as if they were chained to two heavy stones.

Everyone seemed to be talking at the same time.

'He fell straight on the rock. The back of his head is shattered!'

'How did this happen?'

'He was plucking mangoes and slipped.'

'Aah! He was such a fine boy!'

'The two brothers were like Ram and Lakshman! Alas, this boy is now without a brother!' someone said, putting a sympathetic hand on Niru's head.

The sounds entered inside Niru's head, growing louder and louder and finally rose to a crescendo. Niru pressed his hands hard over his ears. Suddenly, there was total silence and everything went blank.

ᏊᏯ

I had become an engineer, as my father had desired. He was very happy when I got the job. 'I am happy because all of you are happy,' my mother said. Three years after my marriage, my younger sister was married into a good family. My parents stayed with me, barring a few occasions when their presence was needed in the village or when I got posted to some distant place. They had settled permanently in Bhubaneswar after I got my posting there. They were getting old and I couldn't let them live alone and uncared for in the village. Meanwhile, the husband of Kuni, my younger sister, also got a transfer to Bhubaneswar. All the members of my family were now living in the same city and we met often. My sister visited my home every week and spent a few hours with us. In short, we were enjoying each other's company. My parents doted on both my sons. But as fate would have it, my father suffered a heart stroke and died prematurely. My younger son was just five then. Mother was drawn to my sons more and more after my father's death. She treated them more as her sons than as grandsons. She would never let them out of their sight. Lata and I considered ourselves fortunate that our children received so much love and attention from their grandma. These days, most children live abroad and are not able to even see their grandparents. Where could have my sons found such love and concern once they grew up?

It was a Sunday afternoon. My sister and her husband had come to our home, as they did on most other Sundays. After a sumptuous lunch, we sat relaxing in the living room, talking randomly. My wife, Lata, was preparing to get up and go to the kitchen to make tea but could not tear herself away from the gossip.

Mother walked into the room briskly. She usually takes a short nap after her lunch. We did not expect her at this hour and looked at her in mild surprise. She seemed to be pulling someone by his hand. The end of her white sari trailed along the floor. I leant out a little to see whom she was pulling. My elder son stood behind the door curtain. He was a shy boy and hesitated to come in. But Mother looked happy. 'You know, Kuni,' she said excitedly to my sister. 'Our Debu has got a gold medal in the swimming event. Debu, come here and show the medal to your aunt and uncle.' She turned to look at Lata and me. 'Daughter-in-law, do not let the boy go out alone at noon. He goes swimming, but it isn't safe! Somebody might cast an evil eye on the child. Anything can happen!' Mother turned to my son, and said, 'Debu, my child, my darling! You must never go out without telling anyone.'

My son was still hidden behind the curtain. All four of us stopped talking and looked at Mother. She looked calm and absolutely normal. For a moment or so, there was total silence in the room.

My elder son, who had won the gold medal for swimming, is named Saurindra, but we call him Pupun.

The name of my deceased elder brother was Debendra. However, to my parents, he was Debu—the name by which my mother had called Pupun.

The N-Club

The three of them, Neelima, Neerad, and Nirmal, reminisced over the little incidents of the past and laughed merrily as the big car sped along the Delhi–Jaipur highway. Small things are often blown out of proportion when one is young. The first amusing memory that came to their minds was that of the 'N-Club'. They had been in the same tutorial group when in college, and suddenly, one day, it dawned on one of them that the names of all three began with the letter 'N'. Was that what had brought them together? They were seen in each other's company nearly always. 'Here come the members of the "N- Club",' other students used to tease them as they roamed together through the college corridors. The three took these jokes lightly. Even after they had left college, they used to write 'N-Club' at the top of the page whenever they wrote letters to each other.

'Really, Neerad,' Neelima said, looking at him, 'it's hard to imagine you are a famous advocate now! I have no doubt you must be eloquent in your arguments—and to think that you were so shy in those days! You even stammered at times. Do you still stumble on words while defending your clients?' she asked.

'What a question!' Nirmal broke in without giving Neerad a
chance to reply. 'I'm sure he doesn't even stumble on his own
conscience as he prepares his bogus arguments for the judge!'

'Look who's talking!' Neerad said. 'I seem to remember
that you used to get your chappals made out of old truck tyres
to prove you were a true Gandhian! And just look at your
footwear now! Designer shoes! Your son studies in the United
States and you ride in a Honda Accord! You must be claiming
your share of loot from contractors before passing their bills!
I should file a public interest litigation case against all you
corrupt bureaucrats!'

'Hold it!' Neelima intervened. 'Can't you two give up your
old habits? Just five minutes together and you start a fight!
Tell me one thing, how did you manage to avoid these quarrels
when I wasn't around to play the referee?'

'On the contrary, Neelima, we have resumed our fight only
because you are here to light the fire!' Neerad said. 'Otherwise,
we are the best of friends when we meet, once or twice a year.'

They scarcely found the time to exchange pleasantries now,
let alone pick quarrels with each other. Life gripped them too
securely to allow any respite.

It was a long time since they had travelled together like
this, recalling happy memories of days now lost in the haze of
time. Too many things had happened in between. All of them
had crossed fifty-five. A wide river of time separated them
from their memories. But there were moments such as these
when time appeared to reverse its flow.

Neelima looked through the window. Nirmal asked the
driver to lower the volume of the stereo and Neerad seemed
to have dozed off.

Years ago, they had studied at the same university. Those were the days of dreams and promises.

They existed only in the memory now. Time had twisted their dreams into shapes of its own choice.

Neelima had left for the United States with her engineer husband immediately after her marriage. She had joined a university there after doing her doctorate. The other two lived in Delhi. Nirmal was the managing director of a nationalized corporation and Neerad, a renowned advocate practising in the Supreme Court. All three had prospered. They hadn't met in the last two years but had kept in touch.

It was around six in the evening when they reached Neerad's farmhouse. The place looked peaceful in the light of the retreating sun. There were patches of gladioli and roses; the pond on one side was hemmed around by fruit-laden papaya trees. Neerad led them to the terrace of the small cottage in the middle of the garden. 'Watching the sunset from the roof is an unforgettable experience,' Neerad remarked as they climbed the stairs. The garden looked like a painting. The fragrance of *raat-ki-rani* flowers was wafted to them by the breeze.

Tables were set up on the roof and an array of snacks and expensive drinks appeared. They sat down comfortably on the cushioned chairs and started chatting.

'You've been in America for many years now,' Neerad spoke to Neelima. 'How do you find the life there?'

'Well, there were problems initially but life became easier after my husband got his green card and I found a job. We have our own house in Michigan and we recently bought a second one in Chicago. Besides, we have two apartments here in Delhi. My husband is happy with his job though it involves a lot of travelling. The children are busy with their own lives. We have given them a lot of freedom since they were kids. My son is so busy building up his own business that he has decided to marry late and our daughter has an American boyfriend. I wasn't too happy about that at first but I've stopped thinking about it now. The children have been brought up as Americans, so what harm can there be in having an American boyfriend? On the whole, life hasn't treated us too badly. We are much better off there than we could have been in India.'

She looked at Nirmal. 'Well, Nirmal tell me about yourself. I haven't heard from you for quite some time.'

'Oh, everything is just fine. Both my sons have settled abroad and are doing well. You know how government jobs are. Promotions come regularly and without too much effort. Somehow, I've always been lucky in my postings. We've been in Delhi for the last fourteen years. Maybe I'll get a UN assignment shortly—and then, retirement. We are undecided whether to settle in Delhi or to go back to Bhubaneswar. We'll probably stay on.' Nirmal paused and took a sip from his glass.

'And you?' Neelima looked at Neerad.

'Not too bad—in fact, I never expected to come this far. Do you remember how hard we used to study when we were in college? I always felt it wasn't going to be of much help. I came to Delhi, did my law education, and started to practice here. I learnt the tricks of the trade and rose in the profession. My law firm has grown—we have branches in Mumbai and Bangalore. My son will come back from London after completing his law degree and join the firm. Things seem to be going as planned.' Neerad poured some more whiskey into his glass.

'That's an understatement,' Nirmal teased. 'You wear diamond-encrusted shoes now, isn't that right?'

'And you? Aren't you a big shot yourself? One needs a prior appointment to meet you,' Neerad returned.

They sat in silence for a while. A few stars had appeared in the sky. The crescent moon glimmered softly.

'Haven't we been chasing one thing or another all our lives? Have we ever paused to look back? ... I guess not,' Neelima said as if talking to herself.

'How could we?' Neerad argued, picking up a cucumber sandwich from the plate. 'Would time have waited? Once you are in the race, you have to keep running and that's what we have been doing, although the finishing line is nowhere in sight.'

'And do we even know what it is that we are chasing?'

'Quite true. You can't define it! Sometimes it all feels so unreal! Where are the things that should really matter?' Neelima soliloquized, looking up at the sky.

'Yep!' Nirmal said, his eyes closed. 'I guess we have never tried to go deep into life—just held on to the shell! Has success given us happiness? What if we hadn't achieved anything? Would it have made a difference? At times, I feel so totally fed up with this running after shadows! Even alcohol cannot fill up the emptiness. Four pegs of whiskey and I am still not on a high!'

They leant back in their chairs. No one said anything. Perhaps, in the approaching sunset of their lives, they were trying to define the passion that had made them forget their very existence! Was this the nirvana they were trying to create with the help of alcohol?

'Neelima, do you remember Nira? I told you about her many years ago, when I was doing my probation,' Nirmal said abruptly, as if he had been jerked out of a nap.

'Yes, I think I met her once. But that was a long time ago. What about her?' Neelima asked.

'I met her during my training days at the academy. We became good friends and the intimacy grew. She was of a very serious nature: I have never come across a more cultured person.'

'In other words, you fell for her!' Neerad teased him.

'Not quite, though we were certainly very close. Some of my fellow trainees started calling her *bhabi*. I wonder what she found in me!'

'So the story had progressed that far! But why didn't the hero and the heroine get married?'

'I really don't know,' Nirmal said. 'She came from a reputed family in Bangalore. Her parents knew about us and had no objection to our getting married, but I couldn't bring myself to tell my parents, although Nira asked me a number of times to do so. I came home on a month's leave after the training, before the posting orders came. I had promised Nira I would tell my family everything and get their consent. After a lot of hesitation, I finally told my mother about Nira. She was terribly upset when she heard that Nira belonged to another caste and did not speak our language. "It is difficult for girls with highly paid jobs to find a proper match for themselves. That's why they are always on the lookout for boys from decent family backgrounds and it is usually during training period that the boys get hooked!" my elder sister had remarked in disgust. My father was totally opposed to it. It wasn't easy in those days to contact someone over the phone. I could never discuss things with Nira. My parents had chosen a girl for me and my marriage was fixed up soon after.'

'Why don't you tell us the truth, Nirmal? You were so so charmed by the beauty of *bhauja* that you couldn't resist!' Neerad remarked mischievously.

'And how did you finally break the news to Nira?' Neelima asked.

'I didn't. I couldn't even write, I was feeling so guilty! I got my posting orders shortly afterwards and came to Chandigarh.'

'And Nira?'

'I came to know much later that she didn't join her post and went on long leave. She resigned after a year or so. Later I learnt that she had joined an NGO and was living in some village near Mangalore. As far as I know, she never married.'

'I can never forget the intimate moments we shared,' he went on. 'Nira knew that I usually forgot to drink milk after breakfast. She would stand by the door of my room holding a glass of milk in her hand and wouldn't budge until I drank the milk!' he said, putting down the glass of whiskey. He wiped his face with both hands and looked up at the sky.

'Isn't life strange? The past keeps returning when you want to forget it!' Neelima exclaimed philosophically. 'The two of you left Bhubaneswar and went away to Delhi when our Masters exams were over,' she went on. 'I joined a college as an ad hoc lecturer and it was there that I met Sameer. He was two years my senior—a decent, well-mannered boy, shy and thoughtful by nature. I did not show much interest at first; he was just an acquaintance. Once or twice, we travelled together on the bus from Sambalpur to Cuttack. After reaching the bus stop, I used to get into a rickshaw and he went his way. And then once, the bus had broken down near Redhakhol. I got tired of sitting in the bus and decided to stretch my legs and take a little walk. I spoke to Sameer. We stepped down from the bus. It was late October. The night air felt slightly chilly. We were walking slowly on that lonely road, and abruptly, Sameer stopped and grasped my right hand. I can still recall how his own hand shook! "I love you!" he said— just those three words. I was so surprised! We stood there quietly for some time.'

Here, Neelima paused a little.

'And then?' Nirmal asked.

'Two other lady lecturers and I had taken a house on rent. Sameer lived with his friends in a mess. He used to visit our house frequently. We read poems and stories together for hours while meat curry and rice were being cooked on the kerosene stove. My friends liked Sameer a lot. We used to go out together and our friends kept our affair secret. But it didn't last long. "Who is that boy you are going around with in Sambalpur?" my father demanded. I was usually too scared to open my mouth before him, but somehow, I managed to tell him about Sameer. Father asked me to send in my resignation to the college. My marriage was fixed in haste, and a few months after marriage, I left for the United States. The rest is history, as they say, but somehow I haven't been able to forget Sameer totally.'

'And he?' Neerad asked.

'You are the biggest achievement of my life, he used to tell me. I came to know later that he had left Odisha. Nobody knew where he was. He was the only child of his parents. His photographs appeared in the "missing persons" list in newspapers but he couldn't be traced. He never returned. His old parents are living in a rented apartment at Bhubaneswar. That's all I know!' Neelima rose to her feet. '"He was mad", my mother told me when I asked what had become of him.'

The night grew darker. The caterers had already served the food. The three friends sat down at the table. It was a night of memories. Neerad stood leaning against the parapet wall, holding his drink, his back turned to the other two.

'You've heard of Diksha Bhatnager, the classical singer, haven't you?' he asked abruptly, as though waking from a trance. 'I had gone to Bombay for a lawyers' conference and it was there that we met. She had been invited to sing at the conference. She was beautiful and extremely well mannered. And what a divine voice she had! I met her at dinner after the programme and, on a sudden impulse, asked her for her phone number. I was afraid she might take the request amiss but she didn't and gave it to me without hesitation. She had probably taken a liking to me as well! I met her again the next day and the day after. I postponed my return and stayed on in Bombay for another five days. There was something that seemed to pull us towards each other. We met every day at different places in Bombay at a fixed time. The days passed quickly and it was time to return to Delhi. I had to leave Bombay, though I was determined not to stay away from Diksha. I still remember how painful the sense of loss was as I travelled from the hotel to the airport. I was afraid I might not meet her ever again. It was like I was leaving a part of me behind. I have never again felt so lonely, so abandoned.' Neerad stopped and came back to the table.

'Diksha called me soon after I reached Delhi. She came to Delhi fifteen days later for a concert. We both kept shuttling between Delhi and Bombay for the next six or seven months.' He paused here and lit a cigarette. 'I wonder if all artistes are as mawkish as she was,' he went on. 'Her husband had learnt about our relationship—I don't know how; either Diksha told him about it or he discovered it himself. I was thirty-six and my son was six at the time. Diksha was eight years older. Her two children—a son and a daughter—were sufficiently grown up to guess what was happening. There was no longer any need for the secret meetings, as far as Diksha was concerned. We met at her home whenever I went to Bombay, which was often. I can't believe now that I could have behaved so irresponsibly. Her grown-up children had started addressing me as "Daddy". Diksha was determined to divorce her husband and come to Delhi to live with me. I was put in a difficult situation. How could I desert my family and live with Diksha? My career was on the rise. I decided to put a stop to it and keep away from her.' Neerad took a long pause.

'And Diksha?' queried the other two.

'I came to know later that she had got a divorce and was living in Bombay, alone,' continued Neerad. 'Her children were going to some residential school and stayed away from her. Diksha owned a great deal of property. I haven't heard of her performing in any programme since we broke up. She distanced herself from the world outside and became a recluse. She had deliberately chosen to disappear from the scene.'

There was a long silence. The casket of memories, kept closed for a long time, had split open. The musty smell of the past, released suddenly, spread and sneaked into their successful and complacent lives through the narrow chinks of those unguarded moments.

'They—Nira, Sameer, and Diksha—are of a different breed. We are like everybody else, commoners,' Neerad exclaimed with a sigh.

Colours of Loneliness

'I have a secret to tell you,' Maya whispered in Veena's ears.

Veena, her closest friend, who stood just in front of her waiting for her turn to be allowed entry to the examination hall, looked back, her anxious eyes searching Maya's face.

'Later, after the paper,' Maya replied.

Veena's furtive glance swept over the flush on Maya's face and the tiny sweat beads glistening on her forehead. 'What is it?' her eyes questioned Maya.

Maya gave a light push on Veena's shoulder. 'Move,' she said.

It was the last paper of their school finals. Science had never been a favourite subject of Veena's. The misgivings that crowded her mind were further accentuated by Maya's mysterious behaviour.

The sound of the final bell brought an end to the nervous agony Veena was fighting so far. She stood up as the invigilating teacher collected her answer paper and turned her eyes around to find Maya. She took a few quick steps to reach Maya's seat. 'Tell me, what is the secret?' There was anxiety in her voice.

Maya carefully folded the question paper and kept it in her compass box. She looked a bit distracted. 'How did your paper go?' she asked Veena. 'The questions were all right. But I should have prepared with a little more seriousness, I think,' she said, not looking straight at Veena, as though she wanted to evade her question.

They walked out of the examination hall. Time and again, Veena's questioning glance flickered to Maya's face. But Maya's eyes were fixed on the playground at the front.

School was nearly two and half kilometres away from their homes. Both the girls used to walk to the school and return together. That day, Veena was feeling light-hearted—the examination was finally over! It was as if they had crossed a perilous mountain pass. She quickened her pace to catch up with Maya who strode ahead. 'Wait,' Veena called out to her friend. 'Let's go the temple of Lord Tareswara and offer some *belapatra* to the Lord,' she suggested pointing at the temple on the left. 'The science paper was tough. Suppose we failed! Let's promise a special puja to the Lord to get through the exam.' They walked by the temple every day, and occasionally, they went inside to offer a prayer and some belapatra to the Lord. But that day was special. After all, their future depended on the results of this examination! They entered the temple precincts.

'How about taking a walk around the premises?' Veena looked at her friend and moved forward without waiting for an answer.

It was noontime. The temple premise was empty. As they reached at the back of the temple, Maya stopped. Veena cast a brief glance at her and hesitated. A large champak tree stood close to the compound wall of the temple. Without saying a word, Maya walked towards the tree with Veena close at her heels. 'Take a look and just see if anybody is around,' Maya urged Veena, her face flushed red and sweat trickling down from behind her ears. Veena quickly turned her eyes around. 'No, I can't see anybody. Who would come here in this hot noon?'

'Screen me from the front,' Maya half ordered Veena and bent down to put her compass box on the ground. Veena moved to the side, her perplexed gaze fixed on her friend's face. Maya looked down, her hands moved under the sari that covered her bosom and passed over her shoulder. Slowly, she opened the two lower buttons of her blouse, just above her belly. She moved the sari a little to one side. 'Look.' Her voice was almost inaudible.

Veena shifted her gaze to what Maya pointed at. Her eyes opened wide in utter astonishment. Her lips parted but no sound escaped.

'What is this?' Veena struggled to gather composure.

'No idea—there are a few more like this at other places. But this one is comparatively larger and whiter. It looked like a small dot in the beginning, but has spread out in six months.' Maya buttoned her blouse and adjusted the sari. Tears brimmed in her eyes.

'These are white spots—how have they …?' Veena found it difficult to complete her question.

'I don't know!' Maya began to sob hard.

'Don't you worry, they will go,' Veena patted Maya's back, trying to console her, not feeling so sure herself.

'Promise me you won't tell anyone about this, swear on your mother's life!' Maya demanded. Copious tears ran down her eyes.

'Come, let's go inside the temple once again,' Veena said and walked on. Maya followed her childhood friend, dragging her reluctant feet.

The priest must have left long since. Veena stepped into the lonely interior of the temple and picked up a whole, unscarred wood apple leaf from the top of the deity's image. She closed her eyes for an instant and said a silent prayer before handing the leaf to her friend. 'Here, take it,' she said looking straight into Maya's eyes. 'I have made a wish before the Lord. Chant the mantra "Om *Namah Shivay!*" and touch this leaf to the white spots seven times every day after taking bath. The spots will vanish within a few days. Trust me. I have made a number of wishes to Lord Tareswara and He has granted them all. Just have a try!'

Maya's eyes drank in every word her friend uttered. The bold assurance in Veena's voice filled her with a new hope. As if she was under a spell, Maya held out her hand and took the leaf. She touched it to her head in deep reverence and put it carefully inside her compass box. The tears had stopped.

'Come on, let's go home. I am hungry,' Veena said and both the girls walked homewards down the noon-scorched lonely road.

Those were lazy days of the vacation. The examination over, there was plenty of leisure. Maya and Veena spent their time gossiping and playing games of cowrie. There were long hours of swimming in the village pond. They remained at home in the hot noontime, resting or engaging themselves in some interesting indoor activities. Time and again, Veena would ask her friend through gesture if she was touching the sacred leaf to her spots. Maya would nod her silent assent. The secret was hanging between them. They were extremely cautious not to use words to discuss the topic in open.

The results came. Maya and Veena had passed in the second division, though Maya scored a few extra marks than her friend. On a Monday, the friends went to the temple of Lord Tareswara to offer puja as promised. After the worship, they walked around the temple. Veena stopped at the *Bakul* tree behind the temple and waited for Maya to join her. 'Now tell me,' Veena asked eagerly, 'there is improvement—isn't there?' 'Looks like it,' Maya replied. There was a note of doubt in her voice.

'Show me.'

'There are people around. How can …?' Maya hesitated.

'I will stand covering you on this side. The Bakul tree will screen us on the other. No one can see us,' Veena assured.

Maya's nervous hands unbuttoned her blouse and moved aside the sari. Her eager gaze rested on Veena's face. Veena took a momentary look at the spots and averted her eyes.

'Did you notice any change?' Maya looked expectant.

'Yes, the size has become smaller. The colour too has faded,' Veena answered quickly. Her voice did not hold much conviction. She turned and looked ahead of her so as not to let Maya watch her expression. But her answer seemed to have relieved Maya. She looked happy.

Maya got admission in the science stream in S.B. Women's College at Cuttack. She was strong in mathematics. Veena studied humanities. Both the friends stayed in the college hostel.

Days moved on. Soon it was time for the winter vacation.

Maya was terribly upset. The white spots on her body had spread out to other parts. There were two conspicuous marks, one on her right shoulder and another under her left ear. The one on the right shoulder had lengthened to the back of her neck. Despite Maya's desperate efforts to conceal them under her hair, the spots caught the attention of the other girls. Some of them began enquiring openly about the white marks. But the curiosity in the eyes of the others who did not question her openly hurt Maya more. Maya told her friend about the reaction of her classmates and wept whenever she was alone with Veena.

'We have to let your mother know about this. I think you must consult a doctor and go for proper treatment,' Veena said during their journey to the village. Maya's heart broke. Her future seemed to have banished somewhere in the bottomless depth of dark despair. Unshed tears scalded her eyes.

The next morning, Maya's mother noticed the spot as she served her the breakfast of pancake and jaggery.

'What is this?' The shock in her voice startled Maya and she looked up at her mother, fear and shame trembling in her eyes.

'Since when did these spots appear?' Maya's mother demanded, touching the spot on her shoulder with her fingers.

Maya's reply came in loud, body-wracking sobs.

'Hush, hush,' her mother whispered. There was an unusual secretiveness in her voice. A cloud of consternation swept across her face. 'Go,' she urged Maya's younger brother who stood watching the scene, thoroughly puzzled. 'Ask your father to come immediately. Tell him that it is urgent.' Propelled more by the stern look in his mother's eyes than the compulsive urge in her voice, the boy ran outside in search of his father. He found him sitting on the outer veranda, engrossed in discussion with a few people of the village. The boy passed the message to him and stood waiting.

'What is so urgent?' Maya's father asked edgily.

Her mother pulled Maya close, bent her head to the left, and lifted the hair revealing the spot. Maya had stopped crying. A look of guilt hovered on her tear-stained face.

'What is it?' her father demanded.

'Can't you see for yourself? Look at the white spot—there is another below the neck.' Maya's mother began to sob, careful not to sound loud.

'Ohh!' Maya's father uttered and tried to feel the marks with his fingers as her mother had done. 'When did these appear?' Maya did not answer. 'Where else on your body have such marks come up?' he asked bitterly.

This time too, Maya said nothing.

'Why didn't you tell us about this earlier? These must be there for some time.'

'All right. There is nothing to get so worked up about. The homeopath will come in the afternoon. I think a few doses will cure it.' Maya's father convinced his wife and turned to go. He thought of something and walked back to Maya. 'Are you sure you haven't told anyone about it?' he asked Maya. Maya shook her head in answer.

'Good, keep it secret. Warn the children not to open their mouth on the topic,' Maya's father cautioned and strode out.

A look of consternation hung across the face of Maya's mother the entire day. Maya sat quietly, alone, cursing her fate. They didn't dare talk to each other, as if words, like fine points of needles, will puncture the cloak of warm disbelief they wrapped around the icicle of truth. Neither of them ate. 'What's the point in skipping meals? Didn't I say that we would consult the homeopath in the afternoon?' Maya's father was annoyed.

The homeopath was a man in his forties. Maya forgot the name of the disease the doctor diagnosed after a thorough examination. He handed her two tiny glass bottles that contained white globules of the size of mustard seeds. He advised her to avoid going out in the sun, give up garlic, and take the medicine regularly. The cloud of disappointment that had overcast the face of Maya's mother cleared.

Veena came at noon the next day. 'What happened to today's plan of preparing the chutney of dried mango and plucking of ripe star fruit from the orchard of the Mohanty family?' she asked Maya who sat silently on the veranda and gazed absentmindedly at the sunlight splashing across the trees.

'No dear, the doctor has advised me not to go into the sun. The spots have got to be cured.' Maya smiled ruefully.

'No problem,' Veena said encouragingly. 'We shall go out in the afternoon after the sunlight fades. Or else we shall sit on the temple platform.' Veena turned to leave. The look on Maya's face stopped her. 'Why are you sitting all alone here? Come, let's play a game or two of cowrie.' Veena went inside to fetch the playing board.

In the late afternoon, both the girls walked down to the temple platform. They picked up a few pieces of *ambula* and green chilly to go with it. Suddenly, Veena stopped and pinched Maya. 'Hey, look! There is Ramesh—he comes this way.' She pointed to the roadside. 'His eyes are on you.' Ramesh raced past them on his bicycle. His family was rich. No other young boy of the village rode a bicycle.

'Why should he eye me?' Maya said pretending indifference, her face blushing pink.

'How innocent!' Veena jeered. 'While at school, I have often noticed him watching you secretly. Look, he is coming back!' Veena winked at her friend, laughing mischievously. Once again, Ramesh zoomed past them in great speed. He fixed his gaze in front as if he had some urgent business. Maya looked at him from the corners of her eyes.

'It is you he is after. You are beautiful!' Maya remarked in feigned anger and gave her friend a light push.

'You know it all right. He is interested in *you*, not me.' Veena's eyes sparkled naughtily.

'What's the point—I have these dreadful spots all over my body! Could things be the same again? The homeopath says—' Maya's voice broke. 'Hey, you are being too negative,' Veena said soothingly. 'Am I not keep assuring you that the spots will go away? My mother says one of her friend's daughter ...'

Veena stopped abruptly, remembering the promise she had made to her friend not to tell anyone about the spots.

'Veena, you told your mother ...' Maya looked at her friend accusingly.

'That is no problem at all,' Veena assured. 'Mother will not open her mouth. Actually, my uncle at Cuttack is a medical practitioner. My mother has some ideas about various ailments and their cure.'

The winter vacation ended. The two friends were back in the college hostel. Maya took her medicines regularly and kept examining the spots in the mirror. She could not notice any change either in the colour or in the size of the spots. She was filled with a deep despondency. Every night, before going to bed, she begged God fervently to heal and clear the marks. One day, as Maya dried herself after taking a bath, she discovered a few more white marks on her body. Shocked and surprised, she called Veena urgently to the bathroom and asked her to find out if there were more spots on her back. 'Yes, there is another just in the middle of your back,' a pale-faced Veena confirmed her doubt. Maya became thoroughly distraught. To concentrate on her studies was beyond her power. The white spots that she saw with her eyes and the reflections of the ones that she could not see directly kept prancing about the pages of the book, jeering at her. Maya could sense that her roommates and friends were trying to keep away from her. One of her three roommates, Maya learnt later, had requested the hostel warden to shift her to some other room. The warden had called her and wanted to know about her disease in detail. She advised Maya to consult a better doctor soon. 'Other inmates of the hostel might contract the disease, and there might be more complaints,' she said. The shame and humiliation of the experience shattered Maya.

'The white spots are like ugly, black threads running across the tapestry of my life. Only death can bring me relief!' she said amidst loud sobs that raked her body.

'Stop crying. I'll come to your room and sleep in your bed. That will teach the selfish girl a lesson!' Veena declared, trembling in rage.

The result of the first-year examination was disappointing. Both of them got through just marginally. Veena was not much upset at her results. She was aware that she was not a bright student. But it came as a great shock to Maya. She blamed the spots for her poor performance. Had her mind not been burdened with the disease, she could have studied with more seriousness and secured better marks, Maya thought desperately. She had hoped to study medicine, but the results nipped all her hope. She decided to do her graduation in the same college with Botany as the honours subject. Veena left hostel and went to live at her uncle's, though she continued in the same college. Maya hardly visited her family in the village. Her father avoided speaking to her, and her mother never stopped reminding Maya that no one would marry her because of her spots. The white spots on Maya's face and body had blemished her younger sister's future, she would add. But Maya went to the homeopath on every visit to village and appraised him of her condition. The homeopath was not a man to give in. 'It is difficult to cure the disease but not impossible,' he would claim. 'It might take a long time, but the spots will go,' he said with confidence. He advised Maya to continue the medicine. The spots kept growing in number and size. Maya was a brave girl, but the spots joined together had thrown her out of gear.

She no longer believed the homeopath. At last, following the advice of Veena's aunt, Maya agreed to let herself be examined by Veena's doctor uncle. 'It is leucoderma,' Veena's uncle diagnosed, 'not at all contagious, but not completely curable. One can live a normal life. Medicine could only hold the rate of the proliferation of the spots in check,' he explained. Maya had hoped that the allopathic treatment would bring an end to her agony. But the doctor's words shattered whatever little hope she had had. Veena stayed with her in the hostel that night. Sleep eluded Maya. Long after Veena had gone to sleep, she lay awake, looking at the ceiling. It was like an epiphany—a moment of encountering the truth she had tried to evade with conscious effort. That night, Maya realized that she was not like the other girls; she could never live the normal life they lived.

Veena's marriage was fixed. The graduation examination was drawing closer. But Veena seemed not to have a care in the world. She looked very happy. 'Won't you sit in the final examination?' Maya asked her friend.

'Who cares about the examinations?' Veena replied airily. 'My in-laws say that there is no need for me to continue studies.' Veena was bubbling with excitement. Maya looked at her friend in surprise. Marriage could perhaps never be as exciting a subject for her as it was for Veena, she thought wryly.

The girls in the hostel organized a send-off party for Veena. They danced and sang, waving colourful handkerchiefs, and teased Veena. The merrymaking was carried on late into the night. Standing a little away, Maya watched them with a calm detachment.

Accompanied by Maya, Veena came to the village for her marriage.

൭൭

It was the day of Veena's wedding. She looked stunningly beautiful in her bridal apparel. The dotted designs of sandalwood paste along her forehead, the jewellery, the red, snazzy veil that draped her face, and the fineries she was adorned with gave her an ethereal look. Maya's amazed gaze followed her friend as she came and went from the altar of marriage. After the marriage rituals were over, Maya returned home with her parents. She did not wait to watch Veena's sending off to her in-laws.

As Maya was about to enter her bedroom after washing her hands and feet in the courtyard, she heard her mother talking to her father. 'We are not perhaps destined to celebrate such occasions.' She sounded despondent.

'Why are you so dispirited? Everything is going to be turn out right if God so wills!' Father said encouragingly.

'Do you think so? From what I have heard, this disease is incurable. It can only aggravate.' She heard her mother's voice. 'People are always ready to find fault. I am afraid that finding a good match for Chhaya will be difficult on account of Maya's disease ...' Mother's voice trailed off.

Maya lay awake on her bed the whole of the night, gazing up at the raft along the attic. She left for Cuttack the next day.

Days rolled into months and months became years. Maya had lost contact with Veena. She only knew that Veena was in Bhopal with her husband.

Maya did her postgraduate course at Utkal University. The two years she spent there were eventless. Life followed a routine. Attending classes and partaking in the seminar meetings, participating in the picnics and festivals was part of that routine. In the meanwhile, the leucoderma had spread to most parts of her body. She took the globules the homeopath had prescribed more out of habit than any interest. She watched with a stoic indifference the boys and girls moving in pairs and sitting under the *gulmohar* trees or near the water tank and in the library corridor. The girls in the hostel spoke to her about their affairs. Maya listened to them but made no comment.

Maya returned to her village after her MSc examinations. Her academic activities and other extracurricular engagements did not allow her much time to think about her disease while she was at the university. But within a few days of her stay in the village, she realized that the subject of her disease had gained more relevance that she had ever wanted it to have. She discovered either sympathy or curiosity in almost all the eyes that looked at her. She kept indoors most of the time and helped her younger brother in his studies.

It took almost a year for the results of the MSc examination to be declared. And it didn't help much to uplift Maya's spirit. She got a second class. The lectureship in a college that Maya had aspired for seemed beyond reach.

'I shall complete the BEd course and seek for a teaching job in some school,' Maya told her father.

'That was exactly what I was thinking.' Looking relieved, her father agreed immediately. Maya, somehow, got admission to the Regional Training College at Bhubaneswar. But despite all her efforts, she could not get hostel accommodation. Maya was quite distraught. Then a distantly related cousin came up with an idea. Her brother-in-law Rabi, a widower with two sons, working in the secretariat at Bhubaneswar, lived in a type-two government quarter. If only Maya could adjust in his house till she got a seat in the hostel, Maya's cousin suggested. Maya had no alternative. She moved in to Rabi bhai's small government quarter with her bag and baggage.

Rabi bhai seemed to be quite a gentleman, a good-natured person without inhibitions. Contrary to her apprehension, Maya found it easy to adjust with Rabi bhai and his two school-going kids. Within a few days, she became familiar with the environment and took care of the household matters. She got up early in the morning and made breakfast. By ten o'clock in the morning, she prepared a simple lunch. She readied the boys for school and then went to the college. During the days on which Maya had morning classes, Rabi bhai handled the cooking. Rabi bhai had given her a duplicate key to the house in case she returned early in the afternoon.

Maya genuinely liked living in the small house. She felt she belonged there. She had developed a strong attachment to the boys. They too had grown very fond of her and called her 'Maya auntie'. She did all and sundry jobs at the house with passion. On holidays, she scrubbed the floor and dusted the house. Slowly, as Maya took over the domestic front, Rabi bhai had relieved himself of the household responsibilities.

It was a lovely afternoon. The boys were at the playground. Just when Maya was straining the tea in the kitchen, she could feel the warm breath of someone on her neck. Rabi bhai stood behind, his body pressing lightly on hers. He began stroking her head. 'You are an angel, Maya,' he murmured. There was unusual thickness in his voice. His eager hands moved down the length of her long plait and circled her waist. 'You have breathed a new life into my family.' There was a note of genuine admiration in his voice. A shiver ran down Maya's spine. The air around her became heavy with an exotic smell. Rabi bhai gently lifted Maya off her feet and carried her to the bedroom in his arms. 'Don't worry, I've had a vasectomy,' he whispered in her ears. In the next half hour, Maya was caught in a giant whirlpool of ecstasy. Locked in the strong arms of Rabi bhai, gyrating faster and faster, she was sucked into its abysmal depth, frantically struggling to explore the magic hidden there.

Gently, Rabi bhai released Maya and sat up. Maya rose from the bed and wrapped the sari clumsily about her. She was still under the spell. She trembled as Rabi bhai touched her hand. 'You were making tea,' he said lovingly. 'Go, get some tea for both of us.' Maya, still shivering, walked slowly to the kitchen. That night, Maya lay quietly in her bed, awake for a long time, the euphoria of what happened in the afternoon lingered in her mind. She admitted to herself that in the last few months, she had harboured a secret longing for Rabi bhai. She smiled softly as she relived the events of the afternoon. She was filled with a deep contentment hitherto unknown to her. Slowly, she drifted into a peaceful sleep.

Maya moved her bags to Rabi bhai's bedroom the next day. She began to see herself as the mistress of Rabi bhai's household.

Rabi bhai's sister-in-law, who was Maya's cousin, and her husband had paid a brief visit. Maya had shifted her things to the small living room before they came. But the sharp eyes of Maya's cousin probably detected something. 'Our Ravi is a nice man. I would be happy if you settle down with him for life,' she told Maya while they were alone. Maya felt her ears burning. She stood silently, her eyes downcast.

During the summer vacation after the first year of BEd, the marriage ceremony of her younger sister was celebrated. As her parents had feared, it took a lot of effort on the part of her father to find a suitable match for his younger daughter. The news of Maya's leucoderma always happened to reach the family of the prospective bridegroom before the negotiation progressed. At last, against heavy odds, Maya's father succeeded in getting a good match for Chhaya. Maya took active part in organizing the function. She was really happy for her sister.

Maya got a seat in the hostel in the second year. But she continued to live with Rabi bhai's family. Her parents did not want to be bothered about it, nor did they interfere in her decisions. They probably thought their responsibility towards their elder daughter was over after leaving her in Rabi bhai's home. Maya, too, was not much inclined to mend a strained relationship. She lived in Rabi bhai's home even after her final examinations. The appointment letter came after a few months. Maya was elated and depressed at the same time. She was posted in a school at Sundargarh, far away from Bhubaneswar. She was happy about the job, but the thought of parting from Rabi bhai was too painful to bear. 'It is your first posting, you have to join,' Rabi bhai said casually. Maya was surprised at the reaction. She had expected him to get upset, and she expected the boys would be unhappy at the thought of Maya leaving them. But nothing like that happened. With a heavy heart, Maya left for Sundargarh and joined the school. She wrote a couple of letters to Rabi bhai. But he did not write back.

Maya lived in a small rented house. It was a one-room-kitchen unit, a part of a larger house that the house owner occupied. The room was small and dingy and lacked ventilation. The damp and musty smell that hung in the room made it a dungeon when Maya compared it to the delightfully fresh house of Rabi bhai. But there was no other choice left, and much against her will, Maya reconciled herself to the odds.

After six months or so, Maya received a letter from her cousin. The letter told her that Rabi bhai had married again. The news hit Maya with the force of a thunderbolt. She stopped going to work and kept herself locked in her room, weeping constantly. She feared that she would go crazy. At last, after almost a month, Maya managed to get hold of herself and joined her job. She discovered a strange kind of sympathy in everybody around. 'What a pity,' the look seemed to say. 'As it is, the poor creature is disfigured by leucoderma. And now something terrible had happened to her. She looks so utterly distraught! God help her!'

Maya's brother arrived from the village. He was not able to get a job despite many attempts and lived in the village with his parents. He had been coming frequently to Sundargarh now that Maya was posted there. Her parents seemed to be always in want and sought Maya's help to meet different sorts of expenses. The reasons varied but the need was always the same—money. Maya never sent back her brother empty-handed. This time, he wanted a good amount to start some business of his own. 'I just need the capital, *Apa*, you are the only person who can help me!' he pleaded.

Maya was filled with revulsion at the selfishness of her parents and her brother. 'Why is it always I?' She demanded. 'Why don't you ask Father to sell a patch of farmland and invest it in your business?'

Blood drained out of her brother's face. 'How could you say a thing like that, Apa?' he asked brokenly. 'Could you ever be so unkind if you were a son of the house?' He fiddled the most sensitive cord of Maya's heart. The hurt in his voice disturbed Maya. He was perhaps right, she thought. Had she been a man, it would have been probably easier to handle the humiliation. Without any further argument, she handed him the money. After a long time, Maya came to her village with her brother. Veena was the reason that prompted Maya to come. Maya came to know from her brother that Veena would perform a puja in the temple of Lord Tareswara on the occasion of the first birthday ceremony of her son.

The friends met after a long eight-year interval. Veena looked a little plump and a little matured. It made her look lovelier, Maya observed. Nothing else about her had changed—she was as chatty as ever. She told Maya about her three unfortunate miscarriages. Her husband had taken her to Bombay to consult the top gynaecologists there. She narrated how her mother-in-law tried to persuade her husband to go for a second marriage, and Veena was so upset that she consumed an overdose of sleeping pills for which she was hospitalized for a week. 'My husband is a gem of a man,' Veena told her with great admiration. 'God only knows how anyone else in his place would have taken such things!' Maya stared at her friend unblinkingly, as if she was listening to a gripping story. 'The doctor made it clear that there was some problem because of which the foetus could not grow to its proper size. But my husband had tremendous patience. He valued our marriage more than a baby. And at last, only by the grace of Lord Tareswara, I was blessed with a child. I was so distressed that at one point, I decided to drown myself in some river or pond.' Veena's eyes brimmed with tears as she recounted her painful experience before her closest friend. Her little boy had a chubby face. He was looking at Maya with rapt attention. Maya lifted him to her lap and put a one-hundred-rupee note into his tiny fist. The boy rocked happily, sitting in Maya's lap.

'Hey Babuna, come to me, here, take the sweets.' A woman's agitated voice was heard. The boy got down from Maya's lap and toddled off in the direction of the voice.

'Didn't I ask you not to go near strangers?' the voice came again, deliberately louder. 'Naughty child, he just sits in anyone's lap—even a diseased one's.' Maya looked at Veena. A pale shadow of guilt swept past Veena's face. 'My mother-in-law,' she said apologetically. 'Don't you take that old woman's words to heart. She would never leave me and my husband alone. I can't remain away from my grandson is the excuse she takes,' Veena whispered, casting quick glances at the open door leading to the interior of the house. 'She is the one who advised my husband to marry again. She has no idea how her son coaxes me in the depth of the night to make love to him!' Veena said with sarcasm, her lovely face blushing pink, her delicate lips quivering in a secret joy. Maya marvelled at such revelation and at the matter-of-fact way in which Veena laid her heart out before her. Maya had never experienced such ease about her relationship with Rabi bhai. In fact, she had never shared it with anyone.

'You have taken the right decision,' Veena said, taking Maya's hand in her own. 'For us women, it is always wise to be financially independent.'

Maya did not say anything.

'Are you managing alright?' Veena asked intently, looking at Maya.

'I am okay,' Maya said without much enthusiasm. She released her hand slowly from Veena's hold and smiled feebly. She was not sure how to tell Veena what a cruel game life had played with her in the last few years. She could not tell her closest friend about Rabi bhai. There was nothing left to share. She deserved the deceit, Maya thought bitterly.

Veena returned after a couple of days. Maya too came back to her work shortly after.

She remained at Sundargarh for another eight years. Finally, more by God's grace than much effort on her part or any recommendation, she got a transfer to Bhubaneswar. She was not sure why exactly she had represented for a transfer to Bhubaneswar. Was she expecting that her life would change there? Maya had no answer to that. But it felt good to be back at Bhubaneswar after spending almost a decade outside. The next task was to get a suitable accommodation. For some time, Maya had to commute from her village, but soon an elderly colleague found her a two-room apartment in a three-storeyed house. The apartment was not very big but was airy and spacious. Maya liked it at the first sight. As she unpacked, the picture of Rabi bhai's house and a host of memories linked with it flashed past her mind. Surprisingly, it did not need much effort to drive them away.

The apartment was on the first floor and so there was no courtyard or a garden. But the house had a homely, peaceful ambience about it that Maya found quite comforting.

೦೦

It was Saturday—school was half day. Maya was back home by noon and lay lazily on the bed, trying to take a post-lunch nap. The stringent ring of the calling bell filled the house. 'It can't be Naveen,' Maya thought. She dragged herself off the bed and, adjusting her sari, walked to the front room to open the door, wondering who could it be at this odd hour.

A smiling Veena stood outside the door!

'What a wonderful surprise!' Maya exclaimed, surprised and delighted at the same time.

'How did you find my address?' Maya asked as Veena embraced her.

'Wait, wait, let me get inside,' Veena stepped in, pushing Maya aside. 'Nice house. But I am angry with you, you never find time to remember me!' Veena's voice held a note of fond accusation. Maya's reply to that was a warm smile. She could not think of a better answer at that point of time.

'We are here for the last one and half years. My husband's job is such that he gets a transfer every three years. Another few months and we have to get ready to shift to a new place. You have forgotten me easily but I have been inquiring about you immediately after we came to Odisha. I had no idea that you have been transferred here. I could have got the information from the village but my parents no longer live there. They are living with my brother at Baroda. Incidentally, I came across the son of Pradhan Uncle in the market one day. It was he who got me the telephone number of one of the teachers at your school. The teacher gave me your address. But I had requested him not to let you know about it. And now,' Veena said with a triumphant smile, 'I am here.' She paused to breathe.

'All right, all right, now give your tongue a little rest and sit down. I will get us some tea,' Maya said affectionately and strode into the kitchen. Veena followed her.

'And your children? Which classes they are in?' Maya asked as she lighted the gas stove.

'Children? We have only one son, the one whom you saw in the village. He is studying in the Central School, class eighth. He will be fourteen in the coming October.'

'And your husband?'

'He has recently been promoted to the rank of the chief manager in the bank. We have requested for a posting here at Bhubaneswar. My husband and some of his friends had brought plots here long back. We want to construct a house on that plot. We have to have a shelter of our own after he retires, isn't it? We are in a hurry to get the construction completed before the next transfer is due.'

Maya walked out of the kitchen, carrying the two tea-filled cups in both her hands.

'Is there someone else living here?' Veena asked casually. 'I saw a pair of shoes outside the door, and a bag and a pair of trousers on the cot in the living room.'

'Oh, that! Those are Naveen's. He shares the flat with me. A nice young man, works as a mechanic in a nearby TV repairing shop,' Maya replied, looking into the tea in her cup.

'I thought it was your nephew. It is better to have someone reliable with you than living all alone. But is he trustworthy, and does he pay you for the accommodation?' Veena asked, like an elderly guardian.

'Oh yes,' Maya nodded. 'He came here on an afternoon and requested me to allow him to live here. He was unmarried and no house owner was willing to rent a room to a bachelor. At first, I refused. But he came again and again and almost begged me to adjust him here somehow. I felt pity for him and agreed. He is a decent young man. He helps me a lot and runs errands for me. He eats here only at night. He also pays for the meal and the accommodation,' Maya said with indifference, as if to drop the topic there.

The two friends talked for a long time. They kept each other's telephone number. While taking leave of her friend, Veena made Maya promise to visit her home the next Sunday. Maya looks better now. The blotches were no longer there. They have spread uniformly all over her skin, giving it a soft pinkish tinge. She has gained a little weight, too. She looks like a European, Veena reflected while returning from Maya's house. Poor Maya! She lived her life in utter loneliness. Let her be a little comfortable at least!

She *had been* beautiful in her young days. Yes, she had been, Veena thought ruefully, but not now. The monotony of living a routine life has taken a toll on her beauty. She looked overweight and gross, and her face too has lost its glow. Every new day brings in the same old problems and worries—making breakfast and readying her son for school, supervising the maid's work, attending to other household chores, cooking the lunch, and again making preparations for the dinner in the evening. The next posting of her husband, the higher studies of her son, the marriage of her younger sister-in-law that was getting unusually delayed—so much to clutter her mind. As she keeps planning for the future, her tomorrows give a slip and turn to today and then to yesterday without her noticing them. *My life is a meaningless vacuum*—Veena thought bitterly as she got down from the rickshaw at the front gate of her apartment block.

At about noon the next Sunday, Maya's rickshaw stopped at the Kedar Gouri apartment block. Maya alighted, carrying carefully the packet of rasgola she had bought on her way. Veena took her in her arms, smiling warmly; her son touched Maya's feet. Veena's husband came out and joined his palms in a formal greeting. Maya tried to remember how Veena's husband looked years ago, but could recollect just a faint image of him. In spite of that, she noticed the changes—the receding hairline and the increased weight that gave him a matured look. He seemed to be a reserved character and talked very less during lunch. Both father and son went inside to take a midday nap. Veena cleared the table. After putting the dishes in the sink, she came over to Maya. The friends sat on the sofa in the drawing room.

'You have a lovely house, like one out of a picture postcard. Your son too is quite obedient and well mannered. An ideal family, I must say,' Maya remarked with genuine admiration. Veena's face lit up, but the glow of satisfaction vanished the next moment. 'I am feeling very lonely these days. Life has fallen into a dreary, cheerless pattern. There is no interesting engagement. Sometimes, I think I had better taken up a job like you. A second child might have kept me busy, but you know all about my problem.' Veena heaved out a sigh. Maya did not say anything.

'My husband doesn't find much time to take me out. The job in the bank is very demanding. In all these months, we had just visited Puri once. Leave it, that's my destiny,' Veena said resignedly and looked at Maya. 'Tell me about you,' she said.

'There is nothing to tell about me—you can see everything for yourself,' Maya replied without interest. 'Find yourself some leisure time and come to my house—make it the next Sunday.' Maya looked expectantly at Veena.

'It may be a little difficult for me to go out on a Sunday— my husband and son would be at home. You know how it is ...' Veena hesitated.

'No problem, you can come any day you are free. I teach in the morning school. I am free by eleven thirty every day,' Maya said solicitously.

'All right, I will call you before coming,' Veena said as she walked down the staircase to see Maya off.

A month had passed after Maya's visit to Veena's house.

She called Veena. 'Hey, I am Maya,' she said over the phone, 'Why don't you come over here tomorrow for lunch? We haven't met in a long time.'

'Tomorrow? Is it some special occasion?' Veena asked from the other end.

'No, no—you know there is nothing special in my life to celebrate. It is just that I have some fresh, large prawns that I want to share with you. We shall lunch together and gossip.'

'Okay, I will try. I shall let you know if I can't make it,' Veena replied.

Next day, Maya heard the knock at the front door as she was changing clothes after returning from school. Must be Veena, she thought and opened the door. It was Veena all right. She held a small lunch box. 'This is white gourd cooked in mustard seed paste,' she said and kept the lunch box in the kitchen. Maya shut the door and came after her.

'Lie down on the bed for a while and relax,' Maya said. 'I shall fry the prawns and make the curry.'

'You will start cooking now?'

'No, no—everything is ready. The maid has cooked the rice. She has dressed the prawns and ground the spices. It will just take five minutes to fry the prawns and make the gravy. I shall also fry some *badi* for you. I know how fond you were of it. You just relax'.

'Gone are the days,' Veena said with nostalgia. 'Now I don't care much about what I eat. The choice of my son and my husband has been my priority. The items of their taste are cooked in our house. I have moulded my taste accordingly.'

She went inside the bedroom and sat down on Maya's bed. She could not exactly place it but something struck her as odd, out-of- place. She looked around the room. A small dressing table stood close to the wall facing the bed. Maya's sari and other clothing hung on the clothesline, and the sari she has just changed from lay on the bed, neatly folded. Then her eyes caught sight of it.

On the foot-side panelling of the bedstead hung a man's trousers. She looked closely around once again and saw another trouser in a hanger and a couple of vests on the lower shelf of a wooden rack. It looked like the bedroom of a married couple. Maya had said that a young TV mechanic shared the apartment with her, Veena tried to remember, but why should his clothes be there in Maya's private room? Are they living together like ... Veena did not let her thoughts travel along the track they strived to. Why hasn't Maya ever said a word about it, Veena wondered. Maya's voice came in, startling her. 'Everything is ready. Come on, let us eat first.' Maya came inside and her eyes met Veena's. She noticed the question there. Maya stood silent for a while, waiting for Veena to come out with her doubt. Veena did not say anything. Maya turned to face the door. 'Come soon, the food is getting cold,' she said, trying to sound casual, and came out of the room. Veena came out after her. Maya's empty bedroom palpated with a number of unasked questions. They sat down across each other in two chairs at the wooden table. Maya ladled the food out on to the plates. They began eating silently. A lump of curiosity stuck in Veena's throat, making the swallowing of food difficult. Veena's discomfiture did not escape Maya's eyes. But she did not make any comment.

'Naveen brought these prawns from Naraz,' Maya said, instead. 'Is it good?'

'Excellent,' Veena remarked. 'It's delicious.'

'Don't be so formal. I have cooked it in a hurry.'

'For me, it is a tasty change—I have been fed up with eating the food I cook myself.'

The two friends talked as they ate; Veena told how her sister-in-law was neglecting her mother after the death of their father. Maya said about her own brother who could not do much in life and, time and again, pressed Maya for money. The talks began to revolve around their childhood experiences, and soon they were transported to the wonderful days of the past on the wings of memory.

Lunch was over. 'Let us lie down for some time. I suppose there is still time for your son to return from school. I have some chhenapoda in the refrigerator. We will have it after some time,' Maya said.

'Heh, I won't have sweets. See how much weight I have gained!'

They sat up on the bed. Once again, Veena's eyes fell on the trousers on the foot-side board of the bedstead. She averted her eyes instantly as if she saw something not to be seen. Maya's gaze caught the unease in Veena's eyes. She picked up the trousers and folded it. She placed it on the shelf and returned to the bed.

'Naveen has gone to Berhampur on some business. It will take a couple of days for him to return,' Maya said by way of explaining. She stretched herself on the bed, leaving a wider space for Veena. Slowly, almost reluctantly, like she was trespassing into a forbidden zone, Veena sidled up to the bed. She lay stiffly on one edge as if afraid that her movement might disturb someone else sleeping there.

'I have been living in this apartment for the last four years,' Maya said, speaking to no one in particular, her eyes fixed on the ceiling above. 'At first, I lived all alone. There was nobody who I could ask for help. There was no one even to get medicine when I fell ill. There are some families living here in other flats of this complex, but they keep confined to their homes. You know how it is in Bhubaneswar; there is no neighbourhood here. I am also not very sociable by nature. But life has become easier after Naveen started living here. He helps me a lot and can be relied upon.' Maya paused.

Veena listened in silence, her mind elsewhere. There is only a small wooden cot in the living room and a two-seater sofa. Does Naveen keep confined to the living room only? Veena could not decide if she would want to know more about Maya's relationship with the young man.

'Naveen gifted me this dressing table on my birthday,' Maya began again. There was a latent happiness in her voice. 'Not only this table but the one where we had our lunch ... why do you eat your food sitting on a *peedha* on the floor?

Naveen had said. He has ordered for a bigger dining table,'
Maya said effusively.

'He must be quite younger to you?' The words poured out
before Veena could keep them in check.

'Oh yes,' Maya did not seem to take any offence. 'He
became twenty-eight this August.'

Neither of them spoke for some time. Only the soft whirr
of the fan that revolved above was interjecting the silence.

'A storm raged that evening. Rain poured in torrents,' Maya
said, sitting up on the bed. Veena lay on the bed, gazing intently
at her. 'It was about six or seven months after Naveen came
here. The power went off. I sat in this room in the darkness.
Naveen was in the other room. An hour went by.'

'"Do you have a candle, ma'am?" Naveen asked, standing
in the doorway. "Let me see," I said and groped my way to
the kitchen. I lit the candle and came out of the kitchen. I
found Naveen standing inside this room. All the windows
were shut. The feeble flame of the candle flickered, forming
grotesque patterns on the walls.

'"Would you come here, ma'am?" he said, and before
I could protest, he gently pulled me in front of the oval-
shaped mirror that hung on the wall. Amidst the dance of
light and shadow, my image in the mirror looked at me fuzzy
and blurred. Naveen moved closer to me. He held the candle
in the left hand and something else in the right. Even now,
it gives me goosebumps as I remember what happened next.'
Maya stopped speaking, got off the bed, and drank some
water from the bottle on the dressing table. She stood near
the dressing table and resumed. 'Then Naveen did something
very strange. Even before I could guess what he was doing, he

held the lighted candle in front of my face and touched my face and neck softly with a big peacock plume he held in his right hand. I stood still, my eyes closed tight. Now open your eyes and look into the mirror, Naveen said. I know you won't believe me but I could see my reflection clearly and there was not even a single spot anywhere on my face and neck. Naveen repeated the act several times. Don't think I am lying to you, but I looked exactly the same way I used to look when I was fifteen. Tears streamed down my eyes. I held him tightly in my arms. "Please stop crying, we shall get a new life-sized mirror. You will not even find a single tiny spot anywhere on you," Naveen said, soothing me, and he kept caressing my head.'

'And then ...,' Maya's voice trailed off. Her face flushed crimson. With the end of her sari, she wiped away the sweat that was beginning to ooze out on her face. Veena sat propped up on her elbow, her face resting on her palm, staring at her friend in utter astonishment. Maya stopped. Veena waited, hoping that she would say something more. But Maya didn't say anything more.

'How can you believe it, being so educated? Is such a thing possible in real life?'

'I wouldn't have, had I not seen with my own eyes,' Maya said with emphasis. 'Not just once or twice, I have seen it happen again and again.' Her face still held the reddish glow.

'I am sure that he has an eye on your money,' Veena sounded concerned. 'Is he taking any money from you?'

'No, no—he does the marketing with his money. He has brought all the new furniture and a number of saris for me. It is he who got these prawns for me,' Maya declined firmly.

'Have you ever tried the therapy yourself? Have you ever tried to test the effect of that peacock plume when he, I mean Naveen, was not around?'

Maya shook her head.

'Why didn't you check just for once to be sure?' Veena admonished. 'He might be practicing occultism or some sort of witchcraft. Tell me, where is that peacock plume?' Veena got off the bed with one quick movement and stood waiting.

'I don't know. It must be somewhere along with his things,' Maya replied and turned her eyes about the room.

'Come, let's find it out,' Veena said and moved towards a suitcase kept in a corner.

'This must be his,' Veena said, turning a little to look at Maya, and, without waiting for Maya's reply, sat down before it. The suitcase was not locked. Veena opened it. There were a few pairs of trousers and some shirts neatly folded on one side. Some other belongings of Naveen were kept in an orderly manner. Veena rummaged through the contents. 'Here it is!' She pulled out a big-sized peacock plume from the bottom of the suitcase. Veena stood up triumphantly holding the plume.

'Come on, let's check.' She called Maya. Pale-faced, moving with an effort as if pulled on by some machine, Maya came and stood in front of the mirror. Without wasting time Veena touched the plume to Maya's face and neck. She repeated it a few more times and waited. Nothing happened.

Maya stood like a statue, staring at her reflection in the mirror in utter disbelief.

'Look, can you notice any change?' Veena asked.

The white spots glared back at Maya from the mirror, like they had been doing all these years.

'That boy is cheating you. Watch it. God knows what his motive is. He may try to cast some spell on you or do something dangerous,' Veena said solicitously and put the peacock plume back in its place. Maya was still standing before the mirror, a blank look in her eyes. Veena touched her lightly on the shoulder. 'Be careful. Call me anytime you need my help. You can also come to my husband's bank in an emergency. It is not far.' Veena's voice was unusually soft and cautious.

Oh God, please do not let Maya fall into any trouble, Veena kept praying all the way while returning from Maya's house. She consciously fought off her strong desire to tell her husband about it.

A week after the incident, Veena received a frantic phone call from Maya.

'Naveen has left.' Maya sounded desperate.

'Why? Where has he gone? Has he taken any of your valuables?' Veena's voice was anxious.

'No, no ... he went away—just like that,' Maya said amidst sobs.

'All right, don't get so upset. I am coming.'

Veena hurried to Maya's house. Maya, looking dishevelled, tears flooding down her eyes, stood at the door.

'Tell me what happened,' Veena said, disturbed at the sight of Maya.

'Naveen returned the day after you came here and we ... I had just come back from school and was dishing out the food for both of us. Naveen stormed out of the bedroom, trembling in rage. "Who has tampered with my things?" he demanded. I shrank away from him. I had never seen him so angry.

'"I don't know," I blurted out, thoroughly scared. "Don't lie. Tell me who has opened my suitcase. I will not eat a grain of food unless you tell me the truth," he said stubbornly.

'I did not tell him about you. I admitted that I had taken out the peacock plume and touched it to the spots on my body to see how it works. He became unusually grave when I said that. I kept entreating him to come and eat, but he did not respond. I have no idea when he went away. That is the last I have seen of him.' Maya's voice choked as she spoke. 'I too couldn't eat anything. I waited and waited. But he did not return—not even in the night. I was filled with premonitions. After spending a sleepless night, I called his office at about ten in the morning. Someone picked up the phone and said that Naveen had not turned up at the office. I remained on leave on the next day too. There was no sign of Naveen. Two days ago, I went to school. On my return, I found Naveen's suitcase and other belongings were no longer there. He had a duplicate key to the house. He had come here when I was at school and taken away his things.'

'Is anything missing—I mean money or jewellery?' Veena asked. Maya hid her face between her palms and shook her head.

'Have you called at his office after that?' Once again, Maya shook her head. Both the friends sat in silence for some time.

'I will leave now,' Veena said, holding Maya's hand. She rose to her feet.

'Wait, I will get you some tea.'

'Don't bother. Some other time perhaps.' Veena stopped Maya.

'I will have some too,' Maya insisted. 'It will take just a few minutes.' Maya hurried into the kitchen.

Maya came down to see Veena off. 'One way, what has happened is good,' Veena remarked, taking Maya's hand in her own. 'Something that is not to last should better be abandoned sooner.' Maya did not answer.

A mild repentance kept haunting Veena for a long time. It was perhaps because of her impingement that Naveen had left Maya. Veena felt guilty—he might have lived with her for some more time, maybe lifelong. Poor Maya, once again she was left alone. She didn't get a chance to meet Maya again during the rest of her stay in Bhubaneswar.

Maya's heart denied to reconcile to the truth that Naveen had left her for good. Day after day, she kept waiting for him, hoping that one fine morning he would knock at her door. While returning from school, a feeble hope used to kindle in her that she would find Naveen reclining on the bed. She half expected him to call her in the evening, asking her to keep the front door unlocked as he would come late in the night.

She remembered Naveen on holidays when she cooked something special. She remembered how he ate the prawn-in-mustard-paste curry with great relish and the rice porridge. 'You can cook much better than a professional,' he used to comment. Maya cooked items Naveen liked, kept them in the refrigerator for days, and then threw them away. Sometimes, she saw someone in the streets wearing a chequered shirt like Naveen used to wear and moved closer to him to get a clear view. She was heartbroken to discover that it was not him. She had called Naveen's office a number of times and they said that Naveen had resigned the job. No one seemed to have any idea of his whereabouts.

Maya went to the school as usual, cooked food, and attended to her day-to-day chores. But she felt that something had died inside her. A sense of loss overwhelmed her and filled her with a strange apathy.

Where could Naveen have gone? Did he simply vanish into thin air? In the loneliness of the night, Maya stood before the mirror and examined her bare body. The spots, whiter and more conspicuous, peeped out from behind the glass. Is it true that Naveen did some sort of magic, Maya wondered? The spots had disappeared, and Maya had seen it happen with her own eyes. How? How? She had no answer, no logic to explain that. Often, Maya was tempted to get a big peacock plume and to test if it really worked on the spots, but something prevented her.

Years followed one another. And the face of the city changed. On the vast wooded stretches in and around the city, there came up high-rise apartment blocks. Several families lived in their respective apartments in multi-storeyed buildings. Maya, too, had procured a flat in one such complex. Though she had been promoted twice to the post of head mistress, she forwent the promotion in order to avoid the transfer. She had made up her mind to spend the rest of days at Bhubaneswar. She preferred to continue in the same school as the assistant head mistress. Towards the end of her career, Maya lost interest in the job and took voluntary retirement from service.

೧೦

As Maya jostled through the heavy crowd in front of the Market Building, stepping carefully ahead, a carry bag in hand, she heard someone calling her name.

'Maya!'

Maya swivelled back to see the caller. Her eyes lit up with joy as she stood facing Veena.

'Veena! You are here at Bhubaneswar!' They embraced each other.

'We are here for the last three years. My husband is retiring this December. Somebody in the village told me that you are here but I didn't have your address.' Like always, Veena went on without stopping to breathe. They were still in each other's arms, each scanning the face of the other intently.

'I am here all these years. I haven't accepted the promotions because I did not want to leave this place. Now I am retired and living here in my own apartment. This is all about me. Now tell me about you. Where are you staying in Bhubaneswar? And where is your son now?'

'We are now staying in our own house,' Veena answered. 'Our son is working in a reputed software company in Canada. He is already twenty-seven. His father wants to get him married before he retires.'

Maya listened, wondering how swiftly time had flown away. Veena's son, that kid, is now doing a job in Canada! And he was old enough to marry!

They talked for some more time, trying to learn about each other as much as possible.

'Time to go,' Veena said, breathing out a sigh.

'Come to my place one of these days,' Maya urged, 'There is so much to talk about.' Maya gave Veena her address and the number of her cell phone. Veena saved it in her own.

'What time will suit you?' Veena asked.

'Any time—I am home most of the time, alone. Just give me a ring before coming.'

Veena hasn't lost any weight in these years, Maya reflected while returning home in an auto-rickshaw. *She must be as old as I am, about fifty-six. But her hair has not turned grey; she has dyed it perhaps,* Maya guessed. *Veena wore an expensive sari. And her eyes—perhaps there were dark circles under her eyes, and she looked tired. Maybe I am imagining things, these days it is difficult to see things clearly even with the glasses on!*

Maya hasn't changed much. Her skin now looks a pinkish white—she does not seem to have leucoderma! There were streaks of grey in her hair, but that suits her personality. The failing eyesight does not let me have a clear view of things, Veena thought as she returned home in her husband's office car.

૭๑

Veena arrived at Maya's two-bedroom-hall-kitchen flat on the sixth floor. It was airy and spacious with marble flooring. 'A nice, well-ventilated house you have here,' Veena, said appreciating the flat. 'You are living in between the earth and the sky—and you have kept it very neat, everything looks so spic and span!'

'That's because I am living alone,' Maya returned. 'No one is there to disturb the things.' Both the friends looked at the old photos in the album and reminisced about the past while sipping tea.

After lunch, they came to the bedroom. 'Stretch yourself on the bed and relax,' Maya said.

'We are living alone here. Our son is in Canada for the last two years. Recently, he has sent a photo of him and his girlfriend, Neila. They are living together, but have not yet planned the marriage.' Veena sighed. 'And, how do you spend your time now that you are retired?'

'Happy and free—I read books when I am not doing anything else. There is a lecturer couple living in this building. They have a nice collection of books. I borrow books from them. I have also bought a number of good books myself. I have a good collection of video and audio cassettes and CDs. Some NGOs organize literacy programmes time and again in the nearby slum. People living here in this complex have developed a community culture. We celebrate various occasions and festivals together. I actually enjoy my life here,' Maya explained. There was a note of satisfaction in her voice. The despair and restlessness of earlier days have disappeared, Veena observed and felt happy for her friend.

The calling bell rang. Maya walked to the drawing room, Veena at her heels, and opened the front door. A boy, probably eight or nine years old, stood outside.

'Auntie, don't forget—six o'clock in the evening,' he said to Maya.

'Yes, dear, your mummy and your grandfather have reminded me a number of times. I will be there in time, okay?' Maya smiled.

'The cake cutting is at six-thirty. Don't be late.' 'Sure,' Maya promised. The boy paused a while to look at Veena, and ran down the staircase.

'That was Guddu,' Maya said. 'They live on the floor just below mine. He will always address me as auntie. How can you be a grandma, you don't have a grandchild. That is his logic,' Maya explained.

'Wait, I shall get you something special.' Maya moved to a small cabinet built into the wall. She took out a bottle containing an orange-gold liquid and two small artistically shaped glasses. She poured a little of the liquid into both the glasses and handed one to Veena. 'Taste it. It is a digestive.'

'Hey, this is wine!' Veena spurted out in shock.

'Not wine—call it a potion divine, it relaxes your mind,' Maya said without any inhibition.

'Where did you get it from?' Veena asked—yet to get over her surprise.

'It is imported stuff. Guddu's grandfather, Mr Mishra, gifted it to me. He was an executive in some multinational company and has retired recently. A widower, he lives with his son and daughter-in-law here. A nice gentleman,' Maya said approvingly. 'He will never forget to call me for the morning walk and get me Tecoma flowers from the small garden by the gate for the puja.'

Veena kept gazing at Maya. A woman can always find a companion in a man at any age, she guessed.

'Here, take a little, just to taste,' Maya requested.

'No, no,' Veena refused. 'I have always dissuaded my husband not to touch alcohol.'

'Why did you do that?' Maya asked.

Veena thought for a while, trying to find out a plausible reason. 'It is bad stuff. Has an adverse effect on health ...' she replied, not sounding too convincing.

'Don't we fall sick otherwise?' Maya said smiling. But she did not force Veena to give her company.

Veena sat silently, watching Maya sipping the golden liquid. After a long time, she spoke—her voice was almost inaudible. 'These days, we are living like two strangers.'

Maya cast a questioning glance at Veena.

'We no longer live as husband and wife—we have hardly spoken to each other in the last two years. Most of the communications are made either through the servants or signs.' Veena took a pause and went on. 'He always returned home late. There was no one whom I could have asked what kept him so long in the bank. The driver once told me that he frequently visited a young widow who was a clerk in the bank. My husband simply evaded the subject. "Don't be absurd. There is no such thing," he would say and dismiss the topic. That's why I was reluctant to come to Bhubaneswar this time. But he insisted—we have to live here permanently after my retirement. It will be easier for us if we get acquainted with the environment. I doubt that he is still in touch with that whore.' Veena's voice was loaded with contempt. She looked pale and drained out. Maya probably did not expect such kind of an outburst from Veena. She wondered what she could say to console her.

'To part from someone dear to you, to lose something you value a lot, to cast aside memories you cherished with care—aren't these the most important truths of life?' Veena asked, her face half turned towards Maya.

'There are other equally important truths too—to make a fresh start, to salvage your dreams from the ruins, to explore new possibilities instead of brooding over what is lost,' Maya responded.

Both women stood by the balcony resting their hands on its rail, gazing at the distant jungle. The fading light of the departing day swept across their elderly bodies, revealing to them their own minds, now shaped to maturity after being cast in the mould of their separate experiences. The soft, cool breeze that rustled past them stirred the curiosity and the regret of leaving a path of life untrodden—familiar to one and an enigma to the other.

'So many years have passed,' Veena muttered, her eyes on the distant forest that was beginning to melt into the darkness. 'Sometimes I wonder if there was at all any need of living all these years. Had it ever mattered if I was not born! Nothing will change even if I die now!'

'Right,' Maya agreed. 'There is nothing special on this earth which I will miss. But I have to live the life granted to me, till the end.' Her gaze too was fixed on the distant skyline.

'Can I come to your place sometimes? I love your home,' Veena said, turning towards Maya.

'Consider it your own place,' Maya replied fondly. 'You are always welcome.'

Glossary

alana	a wooden clothes hanger
ambula	sun-dried raw mango
anganwadi	a playschool
apa	elder sister
asana	a small mat for sitting on
ashoka tree	a tree that bears crimson-coloured fragrant flowers
badi	sun-dried chunks of lentil paste. Eaten fried
baidya	apothecary
Bandit Queen Meera	name of a thriller book series, popular in Odisha during the 1970s
basti	slum
baula	a very small and intensely fragrant flower
bedi	wedding altar
belapatra	wood apple leaves offered to Lord Shiva
bhai	elder brother
bhauja	brother's wife
bhabi	elder brother's wife

chouthi	the fourth day after the wedding—night of union of the bride and the groom
chhenapoda	baked sweet meat prepared out of cottage cheese, a delicacy of Odisha
chooda	flattened and dried rice, commonly used as breakfast in Odisha
chula	earthen oven
cowrie	a kind of seashell that is used as dice in a particular game
dalma	a stew of pulses and vegetables, eaten mostly in Odisha
dhoti	white cotton length generally wore by men in Odisha in lieu of trousers
didi	elder sister
Draupadi's Swayamvar	mythical ceremony where Draupadi, the legendary heroine of the Mahabharata, selected her husband
ekoisia	the twenty-first day's function after the birth of a child
gamuchha	thin towel made of cotton, generally used by Odias during summer
gulmohar	royal poinciana
havan kund	a small fire pit used in religious ceremonies to which tokens such as grains and flowers are offered to the gods

jeje bapa	paternal grandfather
jeji ma	paternal grandmother
kajal pati	a small decorative box to keep kajal (kohl) used by women as black eyeliner
kusha	sacred grass
maichia	a man with effeminate traits
nani	elder sister
Om Namah Shivay	prayer offered to Lord Shiva, in Sanskrit language
pakhala	a mix of water and rice, slightly fermented, a delicacy and everyday meal of the common people of Odisha
peedha	rough wooden small slab used for sitting on
pitha	a type of rice cake
puja	worship
radha tamal	a sweet-smelling purple flower, wheel shaped, grows in a creeper
rasgola	round-shaped white sweet dumplings made of cottage cheese, a delicacy of Eastern India
sannyasin	female nomadic ascetic
saptamangala	the seventh day after the marriage—a special ceremonial day
satranji	a rectangular cloth mat bigger in size that people spread on the ground to sit on

Copyright Statement

The stories in this volume were originally published in Odia under various publications. Oxford University Press wishes to acknowledge the following publishers for granting us the use of the stories.

Paschima Publications

- 'Wild Jasmine', originally published as 'Kurei Phula' in *Kurei Phula* (2009)
- 'The Nowhere Nest', originally published as 'Chadhei' in *Kurei Phula* (2009)
- 'A Real Diamond!', originally published as 'Heera – Mati' in *Kurei Phula* (2009)
- 'Jungle Lore', originally published as 'Aaranyak' in *Antaranga Chhala* (2006)
- 'The N-Club', originally published as 'Kadambari' in *Kurei Phula* (2009)

Vidyapuri Publishers and Book Sellers

- 'The Unborn Daughter's Story', originally published as 'Paapa, Punya Baemitikicchi' in *Vividha Aswapna* (1997)

- 'The Elixir of Love', originally published as 'Swapna Hrudaya Satta' in *Birala Rupaka* (2003)
- 'The Girl from a Foreign Land', originally published as 'Videshini' in *Birala Rupaka* (2003)
- 'Her Best Friend Jaya', originally published as 'Sangini' in *Birala Rupaka* (2003)
- 'A Fable for the Times', originally published as 'Birala Rupaka' in *Birala Rupaka* (2003)
- 'Children's Day', originally published as 'Shishu Diwas' in *Birala Rupaka* (2003)
- 'The Ultimate Pay-off', originally published as 'Chalina Janai Go' in *Birala Rupaka* (2003)

Pakshighara Prakashanee

- 'A Shadow in the Mirror', originally published as 'Kshata' in *Prapti* (2012)
- 'Colours of Loneliness', originally published as 'Sathi' in *Prapti* (2012)

About the Author and the Translator

Author

Paramita Satpathy is an influential voice in modern Odia literature whose works have been widely translated into English, Hindi and other Indian languages. In her career spanning two decades, she has carved out a niche for herself. She has seven short story collections, three novels, a collection of novellas, and a poetry collection to her credit.

Satpathy has been awarded the Sahitya Akademi Award 2016 among many others. Her short stories are ridden with reality, novelties, and pathos spreading over an amazingly wide canvas. They deal with almost every sphere of human life and living. There is an evident expansion of empathy and a conscientious attempt to grasp the anxieties of a society in turmoil from the point of view of the marginalized, the lonely, the less loved, and under-privileged.

Her recent novel *Abhipret Kaal* (Odia) is a work of historical fiction set in the period 1920–47, the last phase of freedom struggle in Odisha. Satpathy joined Indian Revenue Service in 1989 and is presently working as Commissioner of Income Tax in New Delhi.

Translator

Snehaprava Das retired as a reader in English from BA Government College, Berhampur, Odisha. She has translated several works from Odia to English, as well as English to Odia, including *Padmamali* by Umesh Chandra Sarkar, the first Odia novel. Several stories by prominent Odia writers, translated by Das, have been published in various literary journals and magazines. She has translated of *One Thousand Days in a Refrigerator: Stories* (2016) by Manoj Kumar Panda.

As a translator, Das believes that an honest and accurate depiction of the mood and the spirit of the original text is essential for any translation. She has also written a number of poems, dealing with a broad spectrum of subjects ranging from social issues and human values to personal sentiments.